Sonia Corrêa, DAWN Research Coordinator on Population and Reproductive Rights, is a Brazilian researcher and activist. She is a founder of SOS Corpo, Gênero, Cidadania (Recife) and presently coordinates the Research and Political Action Unit of IBASE (Rio de Janeiro). She is also a member of the Brazilian Commission on Citizenship and Reproduction Executive Board. In 1991, Ms Corrêa was awarded a grant from the Brazilian Fellowship Program of the John D. and Catherine T. MacArthur Foundation to develop conceptual interlinkages and international networking across the overlapping fields of gender, development, population and reproductive rights.

Rebecca Reichmann is an independent consultant who has lived in Rio de Janeiro since 1988. Dr Reichmann is currently editing an anthology on racial inequality in Brazil and writing a book on race and gender in the political discourse of Brazilian workers' parties and trade union movements.

DAWN (Development Alternatives with Women for a New Era) is an expanding network of women, researchers and activists from the economic South promoting alternative approaches to development. Following an initial meeting in Bangalore, India, in August 1984, on the eve of the Third United Nations Conference on Women, the network prepared a platform document which was used as the basis of a series of Panels and Workshops at the NGO Forum in Nairobi in 1985. The network was formally launched the following year in Rio de Janeiro, where a Secretariat was established.

The Secretariat rotated to the Caribbean in 1990, when a new General Coordinator was selected, and it is due to move to another region at the end of 1995.

DAWN's specific contribution to the achievement of an alternative 'model' of development, which is people-centred, holistic, sustainable and which empowers women, is to serve as a catalyst for debates on key development issues.

In seeking an alternative paradigm for development, DAWN's aim is to develop a framework, based on an analysis of the issues from the perspective of women in the South, for understanding the economic, social, cultural and political processes related to the issue. DAWN's analysis attempts to reflect the diversity of regional experiences and to relate the experience of women at the micro level of the household and community to an understanding of macroeconomic policies and global trends.

Population and Reproductive Rights: Feminist Perspectives from the South focuses on one of three themes selected at an Inter-regional Meeting held in Rio in 1990. The other themes are 'Environment' (targeted at the UN Conference on Environment and Development – UNCED, 1992) and 'Alternative Economic Frameworks' (targeted at the World Summit for Social Development and the Fourth International Women's Conference, 1995).

Population and Reproductive Rights is clearly aimed at the 1994 International Conference on Population and Development (ICPD), and hopes to continue DAWN's path of proposing new, more holistic, feminist ways of understanding the issues.

Barbados
June 1994

Population and Reproductive Rights: Feminist Perspectives from the South

Sonia Corrêa

in collaboration with
Rebecca Reichmann

Zed Books Ltd
LONDON & NEW JERSEY

Kali for Women
NEW DELHI

In association with
DAWN

Population and Reproductive Rights was first published in 1994, by:

In South Asia
Kali for Women, B1/8 Hauz Khas,
New Delhi 110 016, India

In the Rest of the World
Zed Books Ltd, 7 Cynthia Street
London N1 9JF, UK
and
165 First Avenue, Atlantic Highlands
New Jersey 07716, USA

in association with
Development Alternatives with Women for a New Era (DAWN),
c/o Women and Development Unit, University of the West Indies,
School of Continuing Studies, Pinelands, St Michael, Barbados.

Cover designed by Andrew Corbett.
Typeset in Monotype Ehrhardt by Ewan Smith.
Printed and bound in the United Kingdom
by Biddles Ltd, Guildford and King's Lynn.

A catalogue record for this book is available from the British Library.

US CIP data is available from the Library of Congress.

ISBN   1 85649 283 4 hb
ISBN   1 85649 284 2 pb

In South Asia
ISBN   81 85107 91 2

DAWN's vision

We want a world where inequality based on class, gender and race is absent from every country, and from the relationships among countries. We want a world where basic needs become basic rights and where poverty and all forms of violence are eliminated. Each person will have the opportunity to develop her or his full potential and creativity, and values of nurturance and solidarity will characterize human relationships. In such a world women's reproductive role will be redefined: men will be responsible for their sexual behaviour, fertility and the wellbeing of both partners. Child care will be shared by men, women and society as a whole.

We want a world where the massive resources now used in the production of the means of destruction will be diverted to areas where they will help to relieve oppression both inside and outside the home. This technological revolution will eliminate disease and hunger, and give women means for the safe control of their lives, health, sexuality and fertility.

We want a world where all institutions are open to participatory democratic processes, where women share in determining priorities and making decisions. This political environment will provide enabling social conditions that respect women's and men's physical integrity and the security of their persons in every dimension of their lives.

Contents

Participants at DAWN regional meetings on reproductive rights/population

Caribbean
Caroline Allen, Peggy Antrobus, Cecilia Babb, Hazel Cheltenham, Arilita Gumbs, Elaine Hewitt, Carol Jacobs, Elaine King, Joycelin Massiah, Billie Miller, Peggy Rickinson, Audrey Roberts, Heather Stewart (Barbados); Barbara Boland, Denise Noel-DeBique, Grace Talma (Trinidad); Annette Ebanks, Nesha Haniff, Carol Narcisse (Jamaica); Jewel Quello (Belize); Sonia Cuales, Marijke Schweitz (Curaçao); Clara Báez, Dinnys Luciano (Dominican Republic); Nelcia Robinson (St. Vincent); Rebeca Cutié Cancino, Lourdes Flórez Madan (Cuba); Yamila Azize, Sandra Laureano, Isabel Laboy Llorens (Puerto Rico); Clorinde Zephir (Haiti); Clarice Barnes (Montserrat); Monique Essed Fernandes, Hedwig Goede (Surinam)

Latin America
Elisa Jiménez (Venezuela); Neuma Aguiar, Maria José de Oliveira Araújo, Betania Ávila, Elza Berquó, Helena Bocayuva, Sonia Corrêa, Lucia Ribeiro, Edna Roland, Rebecca Reichmann (Brazil); Amparo Claro, Adiana Gomez, Maria Isabel Matamala, Ana Maria Portugal (Chile); Celeste Cambria, Rosario Cardich, Frescia Carrasco, Nancy Palomino, Rosa Dominga Trapasso (Peru); Mabel Bianco; Zulema Palma, Silvina Ramos (Argentina); Maria Suarez, Alma Aldana (Costa Rica); Teresita De Barbieri, Maria del Carmen Blu, Ana Maria Hernández, Sara Lovera, Guadalupe Mainero, Patricia Mercado, Pilar Muriedas, Adriana Ortiz Ortega, Gloria Careaga Perez, Esther Corona Vargas (Mexico); Ana Maria Pizarro (Nicaragua); Cristina Grela, Elvira Lutz, Margarita Percovich, Isabel Villar (Uruguay); Rosario Calderon Echazu (Bolivia); Mara Bird, Maria Ladi Londoño, Carmem Posada, Olga Amparo Sanchez (Colombia)

Pacific
Margaret Chung (Hawaii); 'Âtu Emberson-Bain, Susanna Ounei-Small (New Caledonia), Mary Soondrawu (Papua New Guinea); Anna Luvu (Solomon Islands); Isabella Sumang (Palau); Netatua Fifita (Tonga); Shaista Shameem (New Zealand); Grace Mera Molisa (Vanuatu); Cema Bolabola,

Jenny Bryant, Gracie Fong, Vanessa Griffen, Ruth Lechte, Ana Tiraa Passfield, Asenaca Ravuvu, Salome Samou, Debbie Singh, Prem Jeet Kaur Singh, Claire Slatter, Kerrie Strathy, Tooti Tekinaiti, Makareta Waqavonovono (Fiji); Tererei Abete (Kiribati)

South Asia
Myrtle Perera (Sri Lanka); Gita Sen (India); Sajeda Amin (Bangladesh); Najma Siddiqi (Pakistan)

South-east Asia
Yulfita Rahardjo (Indonesia); Harka Gurung, Noeleen Heyzer, Evelyn Hong, Alexandrina Marcelo, Vanita Nayak-Mukherjee, Meena Moorrthy Shivdas (Malaysia); Claire Chiang, Chung Yuen Kay, Nirmala Purushotam, Constance Singam, Kanwaljit Soin, Nancy Spence, Vivienne Wee (Singapore); Uhn Cho (Korea); Kuniko Funabashi (Japan); Mercy Fabros (Philippines); Govind Kelkar (Thailand); Tran Thi Van Ahn (Vietnam)

Middle East
Amal Abd el Hadi (Egypt); Samia Tabari (Lebanon)

Africa
Almaz Eshete (Ethiopia); Jean Kamau, Catherine Lore, Florence Manguyu, Litha Musyimi Ogana (Kenya); Patricia McFadden (Zimbabwe); Dina Nfon Priso-Jeanne (Cameroon); Adetoun Ilumoka, Bene Madunagu, Adepeju Olukoya, Grace Osakue (Nigeria); Emelda Boikanyo, Navi Pillay (South Africa)

Preface

Development Alternatives with Women for a New Era (DAWN) is a network of Southern women activists and researchers who evaluate the impact of development models on gender systems in the South. In its first book, *Development Crisis and Alternative Visions: Third World Women's Perspectives* (Sen and Grown 1987), DAWN addressed the issues of population policy, abortion and contraception in the context of its analysis of global development. Now, the network presents a more substantial contribution to the field as a result of dialogue and collaboration with other groups and networks that have accumulated experience in this area.

An integral part of DAWN's ongoing critical analyses of development models, this book investigates the intersection of the conventional population field with feminists' critical perspectives on reproductive health and rights. DAWN's analysis of gender and development has been renewed by insights that emerged in a cycle of five regional workshops organized in the context of worldwide preparations for the International Conference on Population and Development (ICPD) of 1994. The meetings took place in the Pacific Region (December 1992), Asia (April 1993), the Caribbean (November 1993) Africa (November 1993), and at the Conference on Women and Population in Latin America, co-sponsored by DAWN together with the Latin America and Caribbean Women's Health Network, which was held in Mexico (July 1993).

This volume draws upon DAWN members' critical reactions to ideas presented during the regional consultations in a preliminary platform document on population and reproductive rights (Corrêa 1993). A first draft of the manuscript for this book was then reviewed and discussed at a DAWN inter-regional workshop in Rio in January

1994. Another vital source of information and political inspiration was DAWN's continuous monitoring of official events and feminist preparations for the ICPD. DAWN participated actively in the ICPD Regional Preparatory Conferences and the Second and Third ICPD Preparatory Committee Sessions. Concurrently, DAWN members were involved in a number of national and international meetings sponsored by women's organizations to consolidate a common international agenda on the road to Cairo.

DAWN has attempted to integrate in this work the contributions of a large number of women around the world. DAWN members brought their insights to the regional and inter-regional workshops, gathered relevant literature and organized the regional opportunities for sharing and reflection. Peggy Antrobus and Gita Sen inspired me with their intellectual and political energy and openness. Bene Madunagu and Vanessa Griffen provided me with fresh and unusual Southern literature on the topics addressed in this volume, and Vanita Mukherjee, Neesha Haniff and Patricia McFadden contributed enormously with reports from the regional workshops. Taciana Gouveia helped me in reviewing translations and bibliographical references. Audrey Roberts and Sandra Edwards guaranteed, in critical moments, valuable infrastructural support. Most of all I am grateful to Rebecca Reichmann, who shared with me the final and extremely difficult task of knitting together the diverse perspectives compiled by the DAWN process, in addition to reviewing my English. Without her support this work would not have been completed.

The writing of this volume has been part of my workplan as a grantee of the MacArthur Foundation Program in Brazil. The MacArthur Foundation (US), UNIFEM and the Jesse Smith Noyes Foundation have also provided substantial support for DAWN regional and inter-regional activities. At different stages of the process, SOS Corpo-Gênero-Cidadania (Recife), and IBASE (the Brazilian Institute for Social and Economic Analysis, Rio de Janeiro) have shared their institutional infrastructure with DAWN.

Given the process through which our analysis has developed, this volume remains open to dialogue. We therefore welcome Southern women's critical reflections about the relevance of DAWN's inquiry to their own experiences.

Sonia Corrêa

Abbreviations and acronyms

AIDS	Acquired Immune Deficiency Syndrome
AIWM	Asia Indigenous Women's Network
CBD	community-based decision
CEDAW	Convention on the Elimination of all forms of Discrimination Against Women
CEPIA	Citizenship, Studies, Research, Information, Action
DAWN	Development Alternatives with Women for a New Era
FDA	Food and Drugs Administration (USA)
FPAI	Family Planning Association of India
HIV	Human Immunodeficiency Virus
IBASE	Instituto Brasileiro de Análises Sociais e Econômicas
ICASC	International Campaign on Abortion, Sterilization and Contraception
ICPD	International Conference on Population and Development
IPPF	International Planned Parenthood Federation
IRRRAG	International Reproductive Rights Research Action Group
IWHC	International Women's Health Coalition
IWRAW	International Women's Rights Action Watch
NGO	non-governmental organization
NRT	new reproductive technology
STD	sexually transmitted disease
UNCED	United Nations Conference on Environment and Development
UNFPA	United Nations Fund for Population Activities
USAID	United States Agency for International Development
WEDO	Women's Environment and Development Organization
WGNRR	Women's Global Network for Reproductive Rights
WHO	World Health Organization
WIN	Women in Nigeria
WPPA	World Population Plan of Action

Introduction: the population and development debate – moments of conflict, moments of clarity

Controversies surrounding population and development are certainly not new, but Malthusian premises have never been challenged so fundamentally by such diverse actors as in the past decade. Ever since 1789, when the Reverend Thomas Malthus first published calculations to demonstrate the impact of population growth on food production, his theories have been regularly revived and re-formulated. Neo-Malthusian ideas have dominated public policy for over four decades. In the post-Second World War period, the world economy experienced a spurt of rapid economic growth that initiated a demographic transition across the South. With improved socio-economic conditions, mortality decreased and population growth became the norm in the so-called developing world.

In an attempt to counter the trend, scientific evidence was mustered to prove that rapid demographic growth would have negative impacts on developing countries' savings capacity, capital formation and public-sector investments, thereby curtailing Southern countries' chances for development. By the 1960s modern contraceptive methods capable of massive dissemination became available. When the World Population Conference was held in 1974 in Bucharest, public policy guidelines already promoted a combination of economic growth and broad publicly funded family planning, through both governmental and non-governmental programmes.

Researchers and policy makers in developing countries reacted against the neo-Malthusian trend by arguing for the transformation of the international economic order and responsiveness to basic human needs. 'Development is the best contraceptive' was registered as the Southern position at the 1974 World Population Conference. Ten years later, however, neo-liberal economists also questioned the neo-Malthusian framework. Influenced by neo-liberals as well as Christian fundamentalists at home, the United States adopted a *laissez-faire* position at the 1984 International Conference on Population in Mexico City. The US position considered population growth as a 'neutral' phenomenon, within the US understanding of development as economic growth fuelled by free market forces. In what appeared to be an 'unholy alliance', the neo-liberal approach to population dovetailed with religious fundamentalists' views on gender and reproduction, particularly abortion.

The population debate in the 1990s is now pervaded by the conviction that population growth in the South is the root cause of worldwide environmental degradation, leading policy makers once again to cite women's fertility as a barrier to development (Committee on Women, Population and the Environment 1993, Shiva 1993, Wiltshire 1992). Preparations for the International Conference on Population and Development (ICPD) in 1994 are founded in this circuitous history.

The presence of both traditional forces and new voices in the 1994 preparatory process has posed palpable risks of setbacks while simultaneously presenting an unprecedented opportunity to transform the population field. Feminist perspectives have led to substantial revisions in the proposed World Population Plan of Action (WPPA) for 1994, despite continuing and fierce resistance. Historically, women's rights arguments have provoked harsh reactions from the conservative population control community. But the last decade has witnessed an even stronger backlash of political and religious arguments against women's reproductive self-determination.

The international feminist reproductive rights movement has openly confronted conservative religious forces. In contrast to family planners, who adapted their discourse and practice to avoid conflict with religious leaders, feminists have criticized the conservative tendency to 'naturalize' reproduction, sexuality and the family (Antrobus 1994a, Católicas por el Derecho a Decidir 1993; Kissling 1992). Feminists view the family not as a naturally isolated nuclear enclave, but as a heterogenous social phenomenon undergoing profound transformations. Today's most striking illustration is the proliferation of female-headed households throughout the North and South (Southern NGO Caucus 1993). Feminists believe that as gender and family systems are socially constructed, they may be transformed to guarantee equality and provide a foundation for women's reproductive self-determination.

In direct battle with the feminist position, the Vatican Delegation to the Third Session of ICPD Preparatory Committee (April 1994) exercised its prerogative as a permanent observer to the Assembly. The Vatican not only obstructed language in the WPPA that supported legal and safe abortion, it also blocked the inclusion of 'fertility regulation', 'safe motherhood', 'family planning' and 'the right of individuals to decide on the number and spacing of their children'. This political confrontation should not be minimized as a phenomenon limited to the Catholic Church. The notions of gender equality, sexuality, reproductive self-determination and a reconceptualization of the 'family' have all posed a threat to a heterogeneous group of political and religious fundamentalists around the world who may mobilize against the feminist framework.

The most recurrent concern articulated by participants in the cycle of DAWN debates was the alarming spread of fundamentalism (Mukherjee 1993). Fundamentalism is not an isolated Southern phenomenon but a global issue. Apart from its specific religious, cultural and political bases, certain features are common to fundamentalism across all world regions. It is always constructed around a notion of purity and impurity in which 'the other' is perceived as intrinsically evil and must be eliminated or 'cleansed'. Fundamentalist discourse naturalizes the family, sexuality and gender relations and excludes women from the public sphere. Everywhere, fundamentalism uses women's bodies as a battlefield in its struggle to appropriate state power. Fundamentalism is not religious, but a political phenomenon with impacts at national and international levels (Reproductive Health and Justice, International Women's Conference for Cairo '94). At the national level, fundamentalist discourse manipulates religious, communal, racial, ethnic and nationalist loyalties as a source of cultural legitimacy while defusing the energy of political movements away from basic needs and development. At the international level, fundamentalism has particularly interfered in the reproductive rights debate.

In the ICPD preparatory process, increasingly vocal fundamentalist forces, bolstered by the Vatican's intransigence, threaten to destroy a preliminary international consensus that has evolved during the 1980s. The still-fragile consensus recognizes reproductive health and rights principles as guiding the current reformulation of population policies. Official recognition of the reproductive rights and health approach to population may be one of the most significant achievements of contemporary feminism.

Women's organizations at national and international levels represent the emerging power of democratic civil societies worldwide who are beginning to voice their interests in international fora. Feminists centre the principles of the reproductive rights and health framework in an articulation of women's experiences of sexuality, reproduction and health and lack of power (Batliwala 1994, Berer 1990b, Germain and Ordway 1989, Sen and Grown 1987). From that starting point, the framework critiques states' and markets' attempts to use science and technology to control women's bodies and challenges the economic and demographic theories used to justify population policies that are harmful to women.

Women have been able to bring those perspectives to the international debate as a result of their painstaking organizing over several decades. In the South, the large majority of women's organizations matured in economically deprived and authoritarian political contexts where women worked with grassroots communities for social change. García-Moreno and Claro (1994) describe how these relatively isolated initiatives gradually consolidated into national, regional and international networks. Despite their small scale and perpetual shortages of financial resources, women's organizations have engaged in constant dialogue with their societies to change sexist attitudes and practices. In settings where political conditions have allowed, women's advocacy groups have managed to influence legislation and policy guidelines to enhance women's health (Ávila 1993, Barroso and Corrêa 1990a, Dixon-Mueller 1993). In nearly all contexts, women have had to confront the powerful influence of international population policies.

In the 1990s, Southern women's organizations will enlarge their role in the international policy arena. Perhaps the best illustration of this new political environment was when global civil society negotiated international treaties in Rio de Janeiro during the UN Conference on Environment and Development (UNCED) in 1992 (NGO Treaty on Population and Environment 1993). Antrobus (1992) has described how during the Global NGO Forum at UNCED the international women's movement found itself caught in the crossfire between the Vatican and the population control establishment.

Preceding the Global Forum, feminist thought for nearly two decades had been developing a framework as an alternative to both the religious and the population field's instrumental approaches to women. The feminist point of departure was simple: human reproduction takes place through women's bodies. Therefore, religious and cultural institutions and the population establishment operate through existing gender systems (Barbieri 1993b). In every human society – particularly in the ravaged economies of the South – women's daily invisible efforts to feed, clothe and nurture their families are the actions that sustain their communities. This reality, 'social reproduction', derives from the gender-based division of labour, which in turn stems from the assumption that reproductive responsibilities constitute a natural extension of female biology (Sen and Grown 1987, Eshete 1992, Manana 1992). In the world's most diverse cultures, the same set of assumptions underlies women's lack of autonomy to make decisions about their own bodies, their sexuality and fertility.

The population establishment has either evaded the topic of women's autonomous sexuality or addressed it as a hydraulic force to be harnessed in the service of population control (Keysers and Smith 1989). Feminist researchers, on the other hand, have prioritized analyses of the power dimensions of sexuality, understanding that even in circumstances where women enjoy some control over economic resources, they still may be 'sexually submitted' to male power (Fabros 1990, McFadden 1992).

In addition to their recognition of the centrality of women's sexuality, Southern feminist analyses of reproduction resist the mainstream researchers' and policy makers' obsession with statistics on fertility rates, food production, economic outputs, saving capacity, capital assets, acres of forests and oxygen emissions. Southern feminists object to claims that complex and gendered socio-economic, political and environmental systems may be managed by applying technical 'fertility control' solutions. Potentially dangerous long-acting hormonal methods such as injectables and implants and, more recently, the contraceptive vaccine, were conceived within this technological framework. Southern feminists criticize the instrumental bias underlying this 'modern' approach to contraceptive technology (BUKO 1993; Forum for Women's Health 1993; Mintzes, Hardon and Hanhart 1993; Shanter 1992; Wajcman 1994).

A similar bias informs the conventional micro-level analyses of fertility behaviour. In investigations of household dynamics, 'rational decision' models are applied which often disregard critical variables affecting women's behaviour, such as the sexual division of labour and the cultural significance of fertility (Dixon-Mueller 1993, Sen 1994). A related problem is the persistence of colonialist and racist biases ingrained in contemporary population policies (Akhter 1992; Brown 1987; Davis 1993; DAWN 1994; Priso Jeanne 1994b; Forte 1994; Scott 1992a, 1992b; US Women of Color Coalition for Reproductive Health and Rights 1994). Religion and cultural tradition, for example, are frequently identified as barriers to the 'modernizing' influences of economic growth and development on individuals – which are expected to lead to lower fertility. Conventional family planning programmes were carefully designed to circumvent cultural resistances by not confronting tradition.

Precisely because fallacies such as the 'traditional versus modern' dichotomy still flourish within the population establishment, some voices have called for 'feminist population policies' (Berer 1990b). Since UNCED, this proposal has generated a great deal of controversy within the women's movement. Opponents cite the difficulty of defining a 'feminist' population policy and warn against the risk of the population establishment's co-optation of feminist language (GABRIELA 1993; Declaration of People's Perspective on 'Population' 1993). As the dialogue continued the international reproductive health and rights movement has mobilized all its conceptual and political strength to influence the Cairo policy debate (Carta de Brasília 1993; DAWN 1993; Haniff 1993; Mukherjee 1993; Women's Declaration on Population Policies 1993; Women's Global Network for Reproductive Rights 1993b; Japan's Network for Women and Health 1994; Institute of Social Studies Trust 1994; International Women's Health Coalition 1994). These efforts have irreversibly altered the population field.

Official policies may no longer promote the narrowly defined family planning and contraceptive services that have been implemented since the 1960s. The proposed World Population Plan of Action (WPPA) now suggests that contraceptive assistance is just one component of a broad reproductive health approach encompassing maternal and child care and prevention of cancer and sexually transmitted diseases. Although the Vatican's power of veto remains in place, the proposed framework also includes women's access to safe termination of pregnancy and humanitarian treatment of women suffering the effects of unsafe abortion. The conventional approach to women's 'status' that advocated female education and employment as a strategy to reduce fertility has now been replaced by the promotion of gender equality and women's empowerment. Women's rights principles and respect for bodily integrity and security of the person are also embedded in the new framework. As it stands, the 1994 WPPA document reflects a groundbreaking consensus among feminists and the international community, going well beyond the basic-needs approach historically advocated by policy makers in the South. If adequately implemented, the reproductive rights and health framework will provide the conditions that would enable women to enjoy sexual relations safely and make autonomous, informed reproductive decisions.

Clearly, Southern feminists support the new consensus emerging from preparations for Cairo. But women's empowerment and reproductive self-determination will not be fully achieved if global development policies remain unchallenged. Global inequalities in resource distribution and shrinking investments in social programmes have characterized 'development' in recent decades (Sen 1993a). Structural adjustment and privatization have been imposed on Southern governments, severely reducing their ability to respond to the basic needs of the majority of people and leading to massive poverty (Antrobus 1994b; Ashworth 1993; Heyzer 1993). Throughout the South, these trends aggravate existing gender inequalities, further impoverishing women (McFadden 1993; Priso Jeanne 1994a; Anand 1994).

Policy analysts predicted that military budgets would be diverted to support human development after the East–West walls fell in the late 1980s, with global disarmament to follow. But this has not been the case. Instead, ethnic conflicts have proliferated throughout the South and new authoritarian regimes have emerged. Armed conflicts – often fuelled by the interests of arms producers and traders – as well as economic crises in the 1990s have spawned intensive national and international migration. By 1990, 20 million refugees – largely ignored by the mainstream media and international community – were fleeing from war zones around the world, and 80 million people now live temporarily or permanently outside their countries of origin. Subject to strict rules governing migrants, clandestinity or open exploitation, women constitute two-thirds of the world's refugees and half of the international migrant population (Phizacklea 1994; UNFPA 1993a). The weakness of international political responses to these situations – where women are particularly vulnerable – is distressing. DAWN members have called for special attention to be paid to the cases of Haiti, Palestine and the inter-group conflicts spreading throughout sub-Saharan Africa. Ironically, in many such settings of armed conflict and widespread mortality, fertility rates are still high and women are targeted for fertility control.

Control over women's bodies is not peculiar to situations of conflict or to conservative religious, ethnic or nationalist forces. Contemporary economic development models also lead to exploitation of women's sexual and reproductive capacities. In recent years, feminist research and empirical data on commercial trafficking in women has poured in, revealing a complex interplay of economic forces and social representations of sexuality mediated by culture and gender systems (Association of Anti-Prostitution Activity 1994; Coalition Against Trafficking in Women – Asia, 1993a, 1993b; Lap-Chew 1994). Although its determinants include the increasing concentration of capital in industrial poles, labour migration and persistent poverty (Sen 1993a), trafficking in women is profitable and viable in all world regions because gender systems and sexuality are universally constructed to exploit women.

In DAWN's view, transforming the population field in order effectively to apply the reproductive health and rights framework is conditioned upon a virtual revolution in prevailing gender systems and development models. Along with their commitment to human rights, women's bodily integrity and reproductive self-determination, reproduction-related policies must be conceived and implemented as part of a renewed human development paradigm that fosters democratic institutions and, most importantly, equitable economic policies.

1 Fertility management policies: past, present and challenges for the future

Retracing history

> I am not sure whether we have any population policies in the Cook Islands, but I know that in the past women have controlled the number of babies using traditional medicine and abortions ... (DAWN Regional Pacific Meeting Minutes).

Nomadic and traditional agrarian cultures have always resorted to self-regulatory procedures to increase or reduce fertility, as a strategy to balance their community size with available natural resources. Historical evidence also suggests that pre-modern norms and social regulations were designed to intervene in reproduction.[1] Therefore, today's state population programmes are not a novelty. What is novel is that in the modern era the scope of the interventions has expanded enormously. Since the eighteenth century, as economic forces were reshaped by industrial capitalism, state–society relations were transformed and 'private' issues became increasingly subject to public interference. This shift was backed by the development of scientific methods of measurement within an environment where researchers and policy makers were gradually convinced that people could be managed as numbers.

The first examples of modern state interventions directly targeting women's fertility were pro-natalist. The cases most frequently cited are nineteenth-century French and German pro-natalist measures, as well as the Nazi/Fascist regimes' strict family rules to 'perfect' the race and to form military cadres in Germany, Italy and Japan.[2] After the Second World War, demographic dynamics in the USA and Europe were characterized by indirect policies promoting women's retreat to the household and the subsequent 'baby boom'.

Pro-natalism has also permeated most Southern countries' national policies throughout this century. In Latin America, for example, industrialization inaugurated in the 1930s required a large and cheap labour force (Barbieri 1993a, Corrêa 1991). Elsewhere, particularly in the immediate aftermath of decolonization, many national governments favoured large populations as a 'nation-building' strategy. As a result, domestic public policies incorporated both direct and indirect pro-natalist incentives that remained in place until very recently.[3] For decades, those policy patterns coexisted with the emergence and dissemination of conflicting premises about fertility regulation.

Beginning in the mid-nineteenth century, feminists, progressive birth control advocates and socialists advocated women's right to reproductive choice as a basis for women's personal and political emancipation (Corrêa and Petchesky 1994, Gordon 1976). But in the same historical context, conservative eugenicist and hygienist groups advocated fertility control among the poor and disabled, as a way of 'perfecting' society. The premises of both camps influenced public opinion and policy debates, primarily in the USA and Europe, but in other regions as well. In a review of the history of the population debate in Mexico, Cabrera (1990) refers to a 1916 feminist congress in the Yucatan which openly opposed Catholic principles regarding women's roles and reproduction.[4] In the same period, the libertarian birth control movement influenced the 1917 Russian Revolution's abortion laws. Cuba's policy of providing safe legal abortions – the only such policy in Latin America – reflects how that early premise echoed for a long time in socialist thinking.

However, after the 1920s the progressive sectors of the birth control movement gradually lost influence (Gordon 1976, Greer 1984, Davis quoted in Roland 1994). The conservative medical establishment, hygienists and eugenicists appropriated the political debate on reproduction,[5] and their hybrid birth control-eugenicist perspective was then disseminated to the colonies and economically dependent regions through a variety of political and institutional channels. A great deal remains to be investigated about this early diffusion of 'fertility control' ideas in the South. But an incipient institutional infrastructure was probably already in place in many countries when, in the 1960s, state-led family planning programmes were incorporated in development priorities.

The Indian experience is an emblematic illustration of this historical evolution. Bhawan (1993) retraces the population debate in the Indian sub-continent from the 1920s to the creation of the Family Planning Association of India (FPAI) in 1949.[6] During this period, controversies about population size and fertility regulation sparked debates in the Gandhian independence movement. Analysing the subsequent period, Batliwala (1993) describes how international pressures and the national food crisis, among other policy developments, led the early 'cafeteria' approach to family planning (advocated by the FPAI) to incorporate more draconian strategies after 1960.

Although an explosive North–South conflict permeated the population debates at the 1974 Bucharest Conference, the Southern critique of demographic imperatives did not restrain Southern countries from rapidly expanding their internationally funded family planning programmes.[7] Surprising as it may seem, developing countries have not been entirely loyal to the Bucharest agenda. By the end of the 1970s, India and China – countries that led the Southern position in 1974 – had already reframed their former policies to adopt clear fertility control measures (Mertens 1993).[8] When the Second International Conference on Population was held in Mexico in 1984, most Southern governments had incorporated family planning programmes in their policies. In some cases states had, in fact, defined draconian fertility reduction targets (Dixon-Mueller 1993).

Given the evolution of policies in the South after 1974, the International Conference on Population of 1984, in Mexico City, could be interpreted as having signalled the definitive hegemony of neo-Malthusian theories (Canadian International Development Agency 1989).[9] But this has not been the case. The final document's sweeping support for public family planning was overshadowed by the political impact of the US position. In 1984 the American delegation – in close association with the Vatican – adopted a neo-liberal view, proposing that international aid for population activities should be trimmed down and fertility management left to the invisible hands of household dynamics. The most cited theories backing this new approach were produced by Julian Simon (in Mertens 1993), viewing 'population growth not as a barrier to development but as a neutral phenomenon'. Although it threatened the funding base of the population establishment, the US position in Mexico did not substantially change the fertility control premises informing the major international institutions (the World Bank, UNFPA and USAID) and national population guidelines.

In the field, the consequence of the 1984 conference was not a retreat from population control but a trend toward privatized services. USAID's 'social marketing' programmes subsidized private investments to distribute contraceptive methods, and in many countries, fees were also established for previously free services. Another trend after 1984 was the population establishment's resort to environmental arguments in their quest for financial support (see Ehrlich and Ehrlich 1990). By the early 1990s, the 'Ehrlich equation' (correlating population growth to environmental degradation) had been widely disseminated to oppose Simon's theories.[10] Thus, the rationale for population control in the 1990s has moved away from a traditional economic development argument to a case for environmental balance.[11] The preparatory process for the 1994 Cairo International Conference on Population and Development has been permeated with appeals to environmental responsibility, yet Southern feminists and Northern minorities recognize beneath the new arguments familiar and enduring racist and colonialist biases:

> The eugenicists (those who would improve human heredity) of the 19th and early 20th century thought that the poor were inferior, and encouraged 'more children from the fit and less from the unfit.' The last proclivity, 'overpopulation' and its effects on sustainable development, is reminiscent of these policies (Declaration of the US Women of Color Coalition for Reproductive Health and Rights).

The establishment of state-led population control strategies after the 1960s represented a critical turning point in the North's long-term struggle for hegemony over the politics of reproduction. Then, in the 1980s, market forces and privatization of services substituted the model of public investment in fertility control. The 1990s may represent yet another turning point, as the international feminist movement reclaims the ethical regard for women's integrity and self-determination that was silenced in the early decades of the twentieth century. Moreover, today's Southern feminist perspective on reproductive rights is modifying the earlier framework by analysing how political, cultural, ethnic and racial factors interact with fertility (Asia Indigenous Women's Network – AIWN and Cordillera People 1993; DAWN 1994; Madunagu 1994; Priso Jeanne 1994b; Reproductive Health and Justice, International Women's Conference for Cairo '94 1994; Petchesky and Wiener 1990; Roland 1994).

These historical and conceptual developments in the population field are reflected in the present world map of fertility management policies. A variety of forces have driven their design and implementation, including the recent decades' shifts in demographic patterns. Although population control interventions clearly prevail, pro-natalism and ethnically based policies have certainly not disappeared. This chapter will explore the heterogeneity of fertility management policies and identify the detrimental effects of population interventions on women's lives.

Today's policies: overlapping systems
State-led interventions

The appraisal that rates are too high followed by political intervention is reported in China, South Asia, Central America, part of Africa (55 per cent of the African population), and in the island states of the Caribbean (excluding Cuba) and Micronesia-Polynesia. By contrast, no direct intervention is reported in most of South America, Western Asia and the rest of Africa. Finally, in most of Southeast Asia, rates are seen to be satisfactory but intervention to lower them is still reported (Amalric and Banuri 1993).

If we search for global patterns in the spread of fertility control programmes since the 1960s, a clear sequence emerges. Latin America and Asia were the first regions targeted for lobbying and donor pressures. Then the neo-Malthusian 'wave' moved to Middle Eastern countries and later to sub-Saharan Africa. In the 1990s, environmental arguments for fertility control have been incorporated in the policy discourse both in the Caribbean and the Pacific regions. Global data on government policies (Dixon-Mueller 1993) suggest that family planning has now become a state-led policy worldwide. Out of the 107 surveyed Southern countries, only 11 do not implement government family planning programmes.[12] As sweeping as the recent institutionalization of family planning may seem, state policies cannot be judged as fully responsible for global fertility decline because, among other reasons, their effectiveness is extremely uneven. Ross, Mauldin and Miller (1993) recently published a statistical compendium on population and family planning (Table 11) in which the efforts of government family planning programmes are scored. Fourteen government programmes are scored as 'strong'; twenty-nine are evaluated as 'moderate', thirty-eight programmes are characterized as 'weak' and seventeen as 'very weak' or nonexistent.[13]

The information on funding sources for family planning in seventy-two countries provided by the same compendium (1993, Table 22) demonstrates that in a few cases fertility management is funded predominantly by national governments: Mexico, Morocco, Turkey, Hong Kong, India, Indonesia, Republic of Korea, Taiwan and Thailand (China is not included in the sample). Funding levels could be considered a criterion by which to evaluate the degree of priority given by governments to fertility control. But even in these cases, differences exist. The Indian, Chinese and Indonesian programmes cannot be simply equated with the less strict Mexican policy or the Turkish programme (the latter is evaluated as being 'weak' by the survey). Many countries receiving large amounts of international population funds are rated as less effective than cases where very limited donor investment is at stake; Pakistan falls into the first category, Chile into the second. In some contexts, family planning programmes considered to be 'moderate' openly contradict explicit double-standard policies targeting certain ethnic groups or pro-natalist stances, as in the cases of Malaysia and Singapore and Guyana. Finally, the eroding quality of population programmes, despite large investments, may be attributed to the effects of structural adjustment (see Van Ahn 1993 for Vietnam data) or bureaucratic incompetence.

Draconian measures implemented since the 1960s certainly explain fertility decline in China (62.9 per cent), and Indonesia (42.8 per cent) but decline has been less pronounced in the cases of India (33.7 per cent) and Bangladesh (29.3 per cent). In contrast, fertility decreased by 49.7 per cent in Kuwait, 28.3 per cent in Cambodia and 31.2 per cent in Bolivia, where no official policies were ever established, surpassing rates of some of Asian countries that implemented heavy-handed fertility control policies. Consequently, factors other than state-led population policies must be considered in our analysis of fertility trends.

Macro-economic forces affect livelihoods, migration patterns, education, and gender systems – all of which have been shown to modify reproductive behaviour. A second critical factor is the historical and ongoing role of the international non-governmental family planning system; and a third element effecting changes in reproductive patterns is, of course, the market-mediated availability of and demand for contraceptives.

The international family planning system

The linkages connecting state policies to an expanding independent family planning system are evident throughout the South. When Dixon-Mueller's data on regional family planning outlets are broken down for 100 countries in Africa, Asia, and Latin America, two conclusions may be drawn (the other regions are not included because the country list is not complete). First, in the majority of countries state-led policies and non-governmental family planning programmes coexist; second, the IPPF network clearly dominates all other non-governmental initiatives. The IPPF network operates in 67 of the 100 countries in the sample, and when local family planning facilities (not related to IPPF) are added to list, the number of non-governmental programmes reaches 77, outnumbering the 71 government programmes.

Family planning NGOs – particularly IPPF associates – were established long before states got involved in fertility control. Parallel to the Indian experience cited above, the rapid expansion of IPPF networks in Latin America was followed by a similar pattern in Africa. In almost every setting, the presence of this international network preceded and influenced – through lobbying and persuasion – the subsequent establishment of state policies. In many cases where local family planning initiatives pre-dated the neo-Malthusian wave of the 1960s, existing milder programmes were adapted to the new demographically driven approach.

Since in many Southern countries family planning initiatives had to confront religious, military and nationalist resistances, their agenda was initially surrounded with a liberal aura. But given the authoritarian political conditions in much of the South during the past three decades, family planners have accommodated to prevailing cultural constraints and profited from the benevolence of authoritarian regimes. For example, Warwick (1988) describes how the National Family Planning Programme of Indonesia adapted to Muslim rules by excluding sterilization and abortion from its guidelines. Throughout Latin America, IPPF associates have used the term 'family' in the names of the organizations in order to avoid open confrontation with the Catholic Church. In Brazil, family planners negotiated directly with the 1964–85 military regime (Barroso and Corrêa 1990a; Ávila 1989).

In a number of countries internationally funded NGOs (mainly IPPF associates) have, since the 1970s, emphasized community-based distribution (CBDs) of contraceptive methods. Among the many drawbacks of this approach, the CBD programmes isolated fertility regulation services from broader reproductive health assistance. When the components of CBD programmes implemented in fifty countries are broken down, it can be seen that just thirteen integrated contraceptive delivery with other health services such as maternal and child care or immunization programmes (Ross et al. 1993, Table 12).[14] In countries as diverse as Brazil and Fiji, these types of non-governmental operations led to a specific pattern of contraceptive use: the predominance of long-acting and provider-dependent methods (Berquó 1993b; Alencar and Andrade 1993; Chung 1992; Bakker 1991). In the DAWN African regional meeting concerns have been raised with regard to the risks of delivering, through CDBs, long systemic methods such as Norplant.

The international family planning system absorbs a significant volume of resources. Financial support for family planning activities rapidly increased after the late 1960s, involving an expanding number of donor countries, although between the 1960s and 1980s the United States maintained its position as the major funder of population activities (Dixon-Mueller 1993). The USA's 1984 decision to stop financing some of the field's major institutions restricted overall funding for population activities, but did not diminish the relative weight of the population establishment's influence on national policies. Recent figures on aid allocations for population and health activities collected by Zeitlin et al. (1994) provide some insights into current finances of the international family planning system.

A small amount of aid is provided to collect demographic data and support contraceptive research, and recently, limited resources from private donors have also become available to women's organizations. But most of the funds support contraceptive services and are channelled to Southern governmental and non-governmental agencies. In the large majority of countries analysed in Ross et al. (1993, Table 22), donor assistance represents more than 50 per cent of overall allocations; in a few cases international resources double or triple the national budget for family planning. Countries experiencing this level of dependency to keep services in place cannot easily refuse population stipulations imposed on international economic assistance.

Resource allocation is a critical issue feminists must tackle in efforts to reframe the population field. Our negotiations preceding

Table 1.1 Population aid disbursements by major donors, 1990 (US$ millions)

Source	Disbursements
Bilateral donors	
(direct bilateral disbursements)	
USA	280
France	143
Norway	26
Germany	16
United Kingdom	15
Sweden	14
Other	64
Sub-total	558
Multilateral donors	
UNFPA	180
World Bank	
(International Development	
Association and International	
Bank for Reconstruction and	
Development)	124
WHO/Special Programme for	
Research Development and	
Research Training in	
Human Reproduction	28
Sub-total	332
Large foundations/NGOs	
William and Flora Hewlet Foundation	2
IPPF	4
MacArthur Foundation	5
Ford Foundation	6
Rockefeller Foundation	11
Population Council	18
Sub-total	46
Total for population	936

Source: Michaud and Murray in Zeitlin, Govindaraj and Chen 1994.

the Cairo Conference have undoubtedly already transformed the conceptual basis of the future World Population Plan of Action. But this leap forward will not automatically translate into revised guidelines for population funding. Chapter XIII (Section C) of the *Draft Final ICPD Document* proposed a budget for the future Plan of Action: of the $11.4 billion investment estimated for the year 2000, $10.2 billion (89.5 per cent) would be devoted to family planning and just $1.2 billion (10.5 per cent) would cover 'reproductive health care beyond usual components of family planning' (United Nations A/CONF.171/PC/5 1994). Those estimated allocations were strongly criticized by Southern countries, Northern governments and women's organizations during the Third Session of the ICPD Preparatory Committee, in April 1994. As a result, the calculations were reviewed and an amended text allocated $17 billion dollars for the year 2000, with $5 billion (29 per cent) for reproductive health.[15] There is no indication, however, that the battle over resources is finished, as the lion's share of funds is still allocated to family planning. The debate will certainly continue in Cairo, but redirecting resources to meet broader reproductive health needs will depend largely on policy decisions taken at national levels.

Contraceptive markets: invisible hands at work
Through DAWN's regional debates it became clear that feminists should pay more attention to the roles of pharmaceutical companies and market forces in providing for contraceptive needs. The subject is not entirely new, as for at least a decade Southern women have researched and protested against dumping of high-dosage pills no longer used in Northern countries. Efforts have also been made to raise awareness about the dissemination of contraceptives which have proved to be extremely detrimental to women's health, such as the Dalkon Shield intra-uterine device, or controversial, such as the progestin injectable Depo-Provera. Present trends require that further research be conducted. As market-oriented policies increasingly dominate the development debate, services will continue to shrink. As we have noted, 'social marketing' and fees-for-services are already

the norm in many countries. A sample of forty-two countries (Ross et al. 1993, Table 13) reveals that ten social marketing programmes were established in 1983 (El Salvador, Jamaica, Mexico, Colombia, Sri Lanka, Egypt, Bangladesh, India/Nirodh, Nepal and Thailand); five more started in 1986 (Bolivia, Honduras, Hong Kong, Pakistan and Taiwan); and another twenty-seven have been operating since the late 1980s.

Subsidized contraceptive marketing alone, however, does not explain today's fertility decline in all cases. If we compare data on social marketing programmes with the figures in Table 1.2, we find that in Sri Lanka and El Salvador – where social marketing has been in place for some time – fewer than 10 per cent of contraceptive users obtain supplies privately. Aggressive social marketing may explain the large number of contraceptive users (up to 50 per cent) served by the commercial private sectors in Bolivia, Egypt, Colombia, Jamaica and Thailand. But the strength of commercial outlays in Brazil, the

Table 1.2 Selected developing countries categorized according to percentage of contraceptive users served by the commercial private sector

≤10	11–50	>50
El Salvador	Belise	Bolivia
Kenya	Cameroon	Brazil
Mali	Colombia	Dominican Republic
Mauritius	Ecuador	Egypt
Niger	Guatemala	Paraguay
Sri Lanka	Haiti	
Swaziland	Indonesia	
Tanzania	Jamaica	
Uganda	Nigeria	
Zimbabwe	Peru	
	Thailand	
	Togo	
	Zambia	

Source: Robery et al. in Zeitlin, Govindaraj and Chen 1994.

Dominican Republic and Paraguay has probably been determined by market forces responding to contraceptive demand.

Global contraceptive sales represent something between $2.6 billion and $2.9 billion per year (Fathalla 1994). Based on this huge economic power, pharmaceutical companies influence not only Southern governments' policies, but the priorities and conduct of health providers as well. Doctors are frequently approached by pharmaceutical companies' representatives, their participation in seminars and conferences is funded by these private sources and, in some cases, they are explicitly bribed. Entire regions are fully dependent on imports of contraceptives, as in Africa, where pills and injectables are manufactured only in South Africa. As purchase of contraceptives by the public sector is still subsidized in many Southern countries, donors may play a strong role in linking government consumers to major private suppliers. As a result, the method mix provided by public health systems is determined not by women's needs but by commercial interests.

Another important issue to be tackled is the formation of markets for contraceptives. Merrick (1990) describes how in Colombia, for example, the wide distribution of pills by the IPPF associate, Profamilia, led to lowering of prices and increased consumption in the overall market (thereby lowering fertility). Worldwide, increasing rates of female sterilization have narrowed the market for hormonals, and pharmaceutical companies have redesigned their strategies accordingly (Fathalla 1994). The decision by Wyeth to request FDA approval of Norplant for in use the USA must be understood in relation to this new trend. The company produces the hormone contained in Norplant, Levonorgestrel, which is also present in the composition of most combined contraceptive pills. For a long time, Wyeth saw no advantage in marketing a rather controversial method which might risk litigation. But the company shifted its position in 1990, probably based on market evaluations detecting increasing preference for long-term methods among American women.

On the other side of the world, the Indonesian government is involved in a joint venture with a Dutch pharmaceutical company to produce Norplant locally. The decision was officially justified by the need to lower the implant's cost for the national programme, but the large Asian market for long-term methods is certainly part of the company's agenda.

Do women want their contraceptive options to be determined by the invisible hand of markets? When contraceptive demand is met predominantly through commercial outlays, distortions may result. Women's options are limited, and they do not get the appropriate information and health assistance to support their method of choice. In circumstances where fertility regulation has been incorporated into women's lives, contraceptive users will often submit to any discomfort in order to avoid pregnancy (Carneiro, in Barroso and Corrêa 1990b). Women will use products that are available, whether or not they are appropriate for their health status, personal needs and future fertility aspirations. Marketing strategies sometimes simply adapt to existing social circumstances, as in the case of injectables. Women's preference for an injectable contraceptive is determined by gender and household constraints, as the method can be used discreetly to avoid conflicts with family members (Klugman 1990). Having detected this market potential for injectables, pharmaceutical companies define their operations as simply fulfilling demand. The logic of the market ignores the following fundamental questions: Would it be possible to transform the constraints posed by gender and family systems? Would it be possible to produce a method adaptable to family and social norms which presented fewer risks and side effects?

Intensive contraceptive marketing generally occurs in settings where strict state regulation, consumer advocacy and penalties for consumer fraud are not in place. In many cases, even when such regulatory mechanisms formally exist, they may be ineffective or inaccessible to poor women. Moreover, given the structures of class, gender and racial inequality that pervade contraceptive options, consumer rights may not be a strong enough avenue to eliminate the human rights abuses that frequently characterize the dissemination of contraceptive technologies.[16]

Trends in today's policies: costs to women

It is not easy to untangle the combined influences of states, the family planning establishment and markets. However, through the DAWN regional debates a preliminary typology of contemporary fertility management policies and consequent demographic trends was identified and will be discussed in the remainder of this chapter.

1. *Fully established state-led policies*: these policies follow the Malthusian model, often implementing draconian measures. In general, governments have been convinced that reducing population must be a component of development policies. In some cases, Southern governments may be subject to pressures from the North, in which government officials are fed elaborate statistics and figures to convince them of the need for population control. The policies are frequently considered 'success stories' in conventional population and family planning literature. The examples most cited are China, Indonesia, India and Bangladesh.

2. *Semi-established or 'incomplete' policies*: this category includes policies that have been in place for a long time but have been only partially implemented, as a result of political controversies, cultural or women's resistances; situations where state interventions are in early stages of implementation; circumstances where explicit population control guidelines are hindered by the dismantling of the public sector in accordance with structural adjustment policies; or mere state inefficiency. Examples may be drawn from most Islamic countries, the Pacific Region and Sub-Saharan Africa.

3. *Combined policies*: this category includes situations in which state-led policies do not fully explain fertility decline. In some cases governments have been only mildly involved in or even entirely absent from direct interventions, but promote and support both the family planning system and market operations. Elsewhere, although 'strong' policies have been implemented, development-related factors may play an equally important role. We will evaluate combined policies and their outcomes in Brazil, Colombia and the Republic of Korea.

4. *Pro-natalism*: explicit official pro-natalist discourse is found

in few countries. But cultural conditions favouring pro-natalism are found throughout the South and often contradict formal policies favouring family planning and population control. Chile, Argentina, Nicaragua and Guyana are the examples we will discuss.

5. *Double-standard policies*: this model is often linked to pronatalism, but in these cases specific groups are targeted for fertility control while others are left alone or provided with incentives for high fertility. Malaysia and apartheid policies in South Africa are clear examples, but the pattern occurs elsewhere and may be intensified in the years to come.

6. *The basic needs approach*: here, fertility decline has been associated with the expansion of education, health services and better economic opportunities for women. Illustrations may be drawn from Cuba and Sri Lanka, where basic needs policies are currently being threatened by an economic blockade (in Cuba) and privatization (in Sri Lanka).

Fully established state-led policies

ASIAN EXPERIENCES   All Southern regions have been touched by fertility control strategies since the 1960s. However, full implementation of state-led population control policies is, in many senses, a characteristically Asian phenomenon. A review of the region indicates that even among Asian state-led programmes, the format, scope and effectiveness of state fertility management varies widely. The most highly visible Asian cases are India, Bangladesh, China and Indonesia. In those countries, family planning NGOs do operate but the role of public programmes is much greater. They have several features in common: the types of contraceptives promoted are either irreversible or long-acting and provider-dependent methods; they often operate in conjunction with coercion or other incentives; and they dismiss women's rights, health status and basic needs.

While mainstream appraisals of Asian policies concentrate on demographic results, the feminist critique analyses different factors, often those entirely disregarded by policy makers, as in the case of

Indonesia. Although Indonesia is hailed as a success story for its performance in lowering fertility rates,[17]

> rarely, if ever, is the programme assessed in the light of its sensitivity to women's needs and desires, or its success in satisfying them ... Targets for numbers of acceptors and current users, often method specific, are set for all levels of the administrative structures which implement the programmeme, down to the village level ... The most alarming aspect of the Family Planning Programmeme is the incidence of coercion. The root causes of this have been identified in the target system, which increases the likelihood of officials at various administrative levels resorting to unacceptable methods of persuasion towards subordinates and towards eligible couples and individuals, in order to ensure the ambitious targets set by the programme are met. Such methods infringe the most basic rights of individuals, especially women (Smyth 1991).[18]

Feminist critiques have also focused on the abuse of women's and men's human rights in heavy-handed state-led policies in India and Bangladesh. While it is true that human rights abuse in the Chinese programme has recently come to the forefront of world attention, the family planning literature generally praises its demographic results. (It is interesting to note that few feminists have evaluated the Chinese policy, probably because of political constraints on access to information.)

In the case of India, since the economic crisis of 1966 the government has promoted the notion that population growth is detrimental to economic advancement. Sundari Ravindran (1993) notes that:

> The Indian government adopted a policy of reducing the birth rate as a way of dealing with the economic crisis of 1966 ... At this time there was pressure from the World Bank to step up efforts at fertility reduction as part of the agreement to overhaul India's economic policies.

The existing government family planning programme was then transformed from providing services upon request to implementing specific demographic goals. As in the Indonesian case, service providers were required to fill quotas, with financial incentives for both acceptors and providers. During its most intensive period, coercive practices frequently resulted in human rights abuses (Batliwala

1993).[19] In the early 1970s, mobile units were dispatched throughout the rural areas to implement mass sterilization campaigns, targeting males. In July 1971 alone, 62,913 men were vasectomized at a single camp in Kerala state. During this period, police round-ups for compulsory sterilization of men resulted in violent riots, and the singular focus on male vasectomies is thought to have sparked protests that brought about the collapse of the ruling party in 1977. Since that time, the government policy has targeted only women.

While international funding to India's official population control programme has been significant since the 1960s, even more funds have become available in the 1990s, in the wake of renewed hysteria over environmental destruction due to overpopulation. Contraceptive use is higher than ever – up to 53 per cent, but the panorama of contraceptive prevalence is extremely distorted:

> Rural women asked: Why are we always at the receiving end of contraception? The majority of methods known to them are targeted towards women and include Tubectomy, Copper-T, Mala-D (the Pill), Diaphragm and Abortion. Condoms are seldom used by men because it reduces their sexual pleasure. Vasectomy is uncommon because of the fear that it weakens a man, thereby reducing his ability to do 'heavy' work, the fear of becoming impotent ... The onus of birth control falls on the shoulder of the woman and is hers to deal with (Institute of Social Studies Trust 1994).

The current aggressive government policy includes support for research on the contraceptive vaccine and Norplant, following the pattern of abuse that prevails in service provision that has been dramatically described by Gupta (1993). In spite of this huge investment, the programme still fails to meet women's need for family planning (18 per cent of all women reponding to one survey said that they wanted to use family planning but did not have access to contraceptives), nor has it reduced fertility in many parts of the country. It treats women as objects of demographic goals, is coercive, operates under sub-standard conditions and provides poor quality of care. To defend its abuses of individual rights, the Indian state uses the rationale of 'the greatest good for the greatest number'.

In Bangladesh, the government has also appealed to the goal of environmental sustainability to justify heavy-handed population policies. The 'green revolution' started in the 1960s to 'meet the demands of a geometrically growing population' is not blamed for today's environmental mess, even though it resulted in eroded and depleted soil and impoverished small farmers (Akhter 1993). The country is a major recipient of international population assistance from a variety of sources, and diverse family planning programmes operate through the public sector, non-governmental services and social marketing programmes. A great deal of feminist literature has discussed the biases and distortions of Bangladesh's population policy (see Hartmann's 1987 landmark study). Their analyses have exposed high rates of sterilization and provider-dependent methods; problems in Norplant clinical trials (Huq, no date); inadequate community-based programmes and devastating workloads of female family planning field workers (Simmons, Koenig and Zahidul 1990). Meanwhile, Bangladesh's female illiteracy rate remains high, the level of gender inequality is alarming in poor rural areas and poverty indicators have not shown any significant improvement over the last decade (Bangladesh Country Paper 1993). Nevertheless, as the decline in fertility has intensified, the country's policy is becoming a new success story. Feminists attribute this outcome to the population establishment's powerful influence on Bangladesh's policy makers. They advocate the transformation of population programmes to respond to basic needs and empower women (Mahmud and Johnston 1994; Hossain and Kabir, personal communication).

THE LATIN AMERICAN EXCEPTIONS: MEXICO AND PUERTO RICO Between 1960 and 1980, while neo-Malthusian theories gained ground around the world, Latin American governments and societies strongly resisted state-led fertility control programmes. Mexico was an exception until a new General Population Law was approved by Congress in January 1974. Demographic concerns had been part of the Mexican state agenda since the 1930s. In 1936, during the Lázaro Cárdenas administration, the first General Population Law was passed in which the peopling of the country was seen as a means to achieve economic and social development, within a nationalist welfare framework. Most analysts identify in this period the beginning of the Mexican demographic transition (Barbieri 1993a). The policy stayed in place for three decades while the Mexican economy was transformed by industrialization.

The 1974 decision was preceded by heated debates between those who considered population a hindrance to development and those arguing that such a policy shift would inevitably result in coercive population control. In the preceding years, more than 100 family planning posts had been established and the social security system began providing women with contraceptive assistance (Cabrera 1990). Both sides preferred to avoid foreign intervention, but the neo-Malthusian discourse that permeated the international policy atmosphere of the period must have strongly influenced the national position. The 1974 Mexican policy is interpreted, even by feminists, as a result of a consensus (Barbieri 1993a). By 1977, the government's demographic goals for the year 2000 were for a one per cent population growth rate. Fertility projections were reached in the first decade, but by 1988, rates (3.8 children per women) were higher than predicted and even stricter goals were set.

The public sector, particularly the social security and health systems, have played a major role in providing access to fertility regulation (Potter et al. 1987). Such expansion was achieved by setting demographic goals for numbers of contraceptive users to be recruited by health professionals. A centralized, bureaucratic and medicalized system has been the vehicle through which fertility decline has been achieved. The Mexican example may not be comparable with the extreme abuses identified elsewhere, however, because other forces were at work in the Latin American context.

But Mexico's policy is not exempt from criticism. Its rapid deprivatization of reproduction did not challenge gender inequality, since, for example, abortion remains illegal (Elu 1993). Fertility has declined in Mexico in a context of concentrated wealth, shrinking wages and deteriorating quality of life for the majority of the popu-

Box 1.1 Sterilization in Puerto Rico: from massive and imposed to wanted and not available

In 1974, a government report acknowledged that by 1968, more than 35 per cent of Puerto Rican women of child-bearing age had been sterilized. Sterilization was introduced in Puerto Rico in the 1930s. However, it was between the 1950s and the 1970s that sterilization became the chief tool of population control on the island. Sterilization was part of an ideology claiming that over-population strained available resources. In those decades, Puerto Rican women who turned to the public health system – those who could not afford private care – were sterilized in massive numbers, many of them without their knowledge. Between 1950 and 1977, the fertility rate in Puerto Rico decreased from 5.2 to 2.7, and it is widely believed that massive sterilization accounted for such a drastic reduction. The indignation and protest of the women's movement, coupled with international pressure, led the government to dismantle the programme. But as late as in 1977, the state was planning to sterilize another 300,000 women.

In 1979, after three decades of abusive sterilizations, the government finally created the mechanisms both to provide information to women regarding the procedure, and to elicit their consent. Waiting periods were established, women were asked to sign a form expressing their approval, and 21 was set as the minimum age to request a sterilization. At present, however, unless a woman can afford to go to a private physician, sterilization cannot be easily obtained. In 1985 and 1986, for instance, the public health system performed no sterilizations, while 85 were reported in 1987 (in contrast to the 25,000 that were performed between 1974 and 1977).

Currently, experience shows that the waiting lists of regional hospitals are such that two or three years may elapse from the time a woman requests a sterilization until she undergoes the procedure. In the meantime, these women do not receive appropriate orientation on family planning methods, and they may either have more children during the wait or abandon the idea of being sterilized altogether. (Edited version of an article written by Sandra Laureano Cartagena (1994) 'Population and Development: We Speak for Ourselves', Panos Institute, Washington.)

lation. Contraceptive use relies on women's primary responsibility for fertility management. The majority of Mexican women, particularly married women and women in relationships, use so-called modern methods such as sterilization, IUDs and hormonal implants. In a period of eleven years, sterilization jumped in prevalence from the fourth method to women's first preference (2.3 million women had been sterilized by 1987) (Barbieri 1993b). The author ends her analysis with the following question:

> Isn't this the time for those of us who are concerned with health and abortion rights, female labor and political participation to rigorously consider the public policies designed to control women's reproductive capacity? This policy provides a necessary service but at the same time for a large sector of the population their free will and freedom are being supplanted ... Are we women not entitled to think for ourselves?

'Incomplete policies'

The arguments dominating the population debate have been constructed to persuade and pressure developing countries to adopt state-led fertility control programmes following the model described in the previous section. However, policies are not automatically translated into concrete programmes for implementation. Also, in some settings, states' adoption of family planning guidelines do not necessarily conform to the population establishment's expectations. Significantly, despite three decades of aggressive neo-Malthusian advocacy, this pattern of formal but unimplemented policies seems to prevail in many Southern regions.[20] The population establishment considers such situations to be a result of 'incomplete policies'. But from a feminist perspective, state-led fertility-control policies that remain ineffective provide insight into policy biases and the complex constraints on women's reproductive decision making. Although 'incompleteness' may be a formal characteristic of recently established state interventions, a variety of long-standing but ineffective policies may form part of the same picture.

ISLAMIC COUNTRIES Dixon-Mueller (1993) provides information about government policies in most Islamic countries: Morocco, Algeria, Tunisia, Egypt, Sudan, Jordan, Syria, Lebanon, Turkey, Afghanistan, Pakistan, Bangladesh and Indonesia, as well as recent reports of limited state involvement in family planning in Iran and Yemen. This list could be expanded to include societies in sub-Saharan Africa, such as Mali and Senegal. In four Islamic countries (Morocco, Turkey, Tunisia and Indonesia), family planning pro-grammes are government financed, and a significant share of international population assistance is provided to Egypt and Bangladesh (Ross et al. 1993).

Through DAWN's debates it has become clear that the rationale for most Islamic governments' family planning policies is a con-ventional development perspective (see also Mazrui 1990; and Mintzes et al. 1993). Since in most Islamic countries population policies coexist with extremely conservative family legislation and communal rules, it appears that the governments have failed to consider the correlations between gender inequality, women's lack of self-determination and high fertility (Patel 1993). In Pakistan, for example, population policies have been in place since the 1970s but fertility decline has been 'weak' (6.7 per cent). Siddiqi (1993) crit-icizes cultural arguments used to justify poor programme results, such as 'people are uneducable'; 'it is a male-dominated and religious society'; and 'women are against contraception'. Her evaluation of Pakistan's fertility control policy suggests that programme shortcom-ings were more significant than cultural factors in limiting women's acceptance of contraception:

> A USAID study showed that for 77.6 per cent of surveyed subjects, religion was not a barrier to acceptance of contraception. Rejection or reluctance was due to unpleasant experiences with the staff and with different kinds of contraception. Women did not dump all methods of contraception, but just went back to the traditional ones ... In 1970 sterilization was offered as part of the population control strategy but not as a service to meet emerging needs of people. Men could choose to be sterilized, but women needed permission.

Tunisia provides an entirely different illustration. The country's policy is classified by Ross et al. (1993) as a 'strong' programme, but its policy rationale is not comparable to the heavy-handed policies of Bangladesh and Indonesia. Feminist researchers (Obermeyer 1993, Hélie-Lucas 1993) consider Tunisian policies as different from those found in other Islamic countries. Women's legal status has improved markedly, contraceptive assistance is easily accessible and abortion is provided on request. Significantly, contraceptive prevalence rates are higher in Tunisia than in Bangladesh. As Hélie-Lucas (1993) points out, such variations reflect the diversity of political contexts determining the quality of gender relations and women's status in different Islamic societies. But some commonalities may be identified throughout the Islamic world. Women's reproductive health status indicators are generally precarious (Obermeyer 1994), and, more recently, spreading fundamentalism means that advances in gender relations and women's reproductive self-determination will be necessarily compromised.

SUB-SAHARAN AFRICA The integration of population objectives in government policies is much more recent in sub-Saharan Africa. With a desire to increase productivity and national development, most African countries adopted pro-natalist stances after de-colonization. As a result, after experiencing increases in fertility between 1970 and 1990, a large proportion of African societies now have high and stable fertility rates.[21] Taken as a whole, the picture portrays a specific stage in Africa's demographic transition. Population is growing as a result of both disruptions of traditional practices and decreases in mortality rates. Therefore, when fertility was declining in other regions in the 1980s (particularly Latin America), the population establishment shifted its attention to the African population 'explosion'. Employing a series of strategies, international agencies have succeeded in mobilizing fertility control objectives in national policy guidelines throughout the region:[22]

Governments and donor agencies continue to see population control policies as a panacea for problems of development. Such policies are heavily donor driven and have used family planning programmes to control women's fertility. Decreasing numbers of people in the continent is the fundamental objective of family planning programmes in Africa (adapted from McFadden 1993).

Although neo-Malthusian discourse has dominated recent policy debate in the region, implementation of concrete policies has not followed. Kenya is one exception: an IPPF affiliate was created in the 1960s and in 1971 family planning was explicitly included in Maternal-Child Health (MCH) programmes. Later, the government defined an explicit population policy. Currently, parallel to the public system, more than 400 NGOs provide family planning services in Kenya. The country has often been portrayed as having the world's most rapidly growing population, but recent data indicate that fertility has declined and contraceptive use has increased. Consequently, Kenya may become a new success story in the population and family planning literature.

Fertility has also declined in other parts of Africa: in Zimbabwe, South Africa, Botswana and Nigeria and to a lesser extent in Sudan, Chad, Central African Republic, Ghana, Guinea, Senegal, Mozambique and Namibia.[23] In most African countries, population programmes are isolated from other health systems and overall development strategies. They adopt vertical delivery mechanisms, and as in the Pakistan example, women may resist contraceptives because of their lack of confidence in service providers and fear of harmful side effects (McFadden 1993).

In Africa, production and reproduction are profoundly intertwined and mediated by gender systems and reproductive and sexual practices (Eshete 1992, Manana 1992). Extended households and fostering of children are intrinsic to the region's cultural and socio-economic fabric (Adams and Castle 1994). From the point of view of women themselves, fertility continues to serve as a fundamental source of status and power within families and society. Women's aspirations for high fertility create enormous ambivalence, as they create a conflict between women's sense of empowerment and disempowerment.[24] In many countries, male political leaders advocate population control but have not abandoned polygamic practices or rejected the social value of large families. And although polygamy is practised in almost every African country, family planning programmes have focused on women, neglecting male sexual and reproductive behaviour (Germain et al. 1994).[25] Some African feminists hypothesize that African governments have not really abandoned their former pro-natalist positions, but simply have adapted to international pressures as a strategy to access increasingly scarce development aid. The states' underlying assumption continues to be that women and fertility are resources to be managed.

The impact of structural adjustment programmes on overall economic conditions and service provision must also be further investigated. Rampant poverty has particularly affected women (Priso Jeanne 1994a), and basic health infrastructure – which was already fragile in most African countries – has been enormously eroded (Diouf and Fatou, no date). Now, in many contexts the only way to ensure the delivery of any type of health service is through the use of population resources to fund existing and new health units. The conditioning of funding in this way seriously compromises the scope and quality of the general health services available. Madunagu's (1993) assessment of Nigerian policies suggests that the cultural and infrastructural barriers described above are not always easy to identify in official documents that are always written in 'acceptable' language:

> The aims of the official population policy are unity, progress and self confidence. The concept of unity refers to tribal division. Theoretically the policy also aims to promote health, well being and a more even distribution of population. Targets have been established for 1995 and 2000 which, in 1992, are far from being achieved. Poverty and insecurity are the main reason why people have large families. Therefore unless class structures and gender prejudices are dismantled, substantive changes in the structure of Nigeria's population is simply impossible.

With Madunagu, African feminists understand that fertility patterns will not change if gender arrangements as well as female productive and reproductive roles are not challenged. African researchers are also attentive to the potential linkages between 'economic hardship and a fertility decline in those countries where structural adjustment policies (SAPs) have been implemented'. If this trend is confirmed, the popular belief that poor women have higher fertility would be challenged, suggesting that 'SAPs function as a population control mechanism' (both quotes from McFadden 1993). In this context, the recovery and expansion of basic health systems is urgent (Manguyu 1994).

THE PACIFIC REGION   Family planning programmes are not a novelty in the Pacific Region. IPPF affiliates have been operating in the region for decades, and public programmes also exist in many countries. Recently, however, the threat of population growth has been increasingly cited in policy debates and new policies have been defined by national governments, particularly in small island states such as the Cook Islands (Pacific Islands States 1993; UNFPA 1993b). Although in conventional population literature the Solomon and Marshall Islands are often cited as the fastest-growing populations in the world, Lateef (1990; 1991) explores little-known dimensions of the islands' demographic dynamics: economic inequality, the disruption of birth-spacing practices, gender violence and land tenure conflicts.

In the Marshall Islands, poverty is increasing and contraceptive use is low (just 8 per cent of women of reproductive age use contraception), but female sterilization rates are surprisingly high among contraceptive users (about 50 per cent). Norplant and Depo-Provera were introduced in 1989. Such a contradictory picture can only be interpreted in the light of the extreme cultural and socio-economic distresses caused by US nuclear testing in the islands throughout the 1950s. Margaret Chung (1991) also stated reservations about the assumption that islands can support only a finite number of people. She questioned whether population pressure alone could be assumed to cause environmental stress in island states. In her view, 'stress' was not just a question of numbers of people, but of economic systems and technology as well. As Griffen observes (1994), reproductive health and rights have not played a role in the region's approaches to population policies:

> In the Pacific, population policy is essentially about control of numbers of children born. Reproductive rights and health are discussed with women as intended recipients/implementers of population programmes, rather than as persons with rights.

Combined policies: Brazil, Colombia and Korea

Fertility declined between 1970 and 1990 in a number of Southern countries that either had no explicit population programmes or very mild policies. The majority of Latin American countries fall into this category. Economic development and a variety of state interventions may have affected reproductive patterns: industrialization resulting in urban migration and transformation of women's occupational patterns; expansion of health networks; modern communications systems such as radio and TV, which reshape cultural norms; and credit policies promoting new consumption patterns (Faria 1989). In addition, an active non-governmental family planning network and effective contraceptive marketing strategies may exert important influences on fertility trends. Mainstream analyses portray the relationships among the above factors and declining fertility as development outcomes, which would confirm the premises of conventional demographic transition theories. But even demographers have been surprised by the pace of fertility transitions resulting from 'indirect policies', and a great deal of research has attempted to explain the trends. However, few have questioned the quality of development interventions that appear to have contributed to the decline in fertility. Moreover, the impact of such interventions on gender has not been adequately explored, particularly in regard to the social costs women may have had to pay.

In Latin America, Colombia and Brazil are countries where fertility has declined rapidly since the 1960s – 60.5 per cent and 55.3 per cent, respectively. Currently more than 60 per cent of Colombian and Brazilian women of reproductive age use contraception. Although government policies have not always been the same in the two cases, the countries' experiences share significant commonalities: in Colombia and Brazil, female literacy rates and women's involvement in 'modern' economic activities have rapidly increased in the last four decades (Merrick 1990, Corrêa 1994a). In both cases, the state apparatus originally resisted implementing population programmes – primarily due to Catholic and other pro-natalist pressures – but placed no restrictions on the operations of the non-governmental system. Also in both cases, comprehensive public health programmes planned in the mid-1980s have not yet been fully implemented (for Brazil see Ávila 1993, Berquó 1993a, Araújo 1993, Costa 1992). Differences between the countries were in spending on contraceptives and in resulting prevalence levels (Merrick 1990).

In Colombia, government and Profamilia (the local IPPF associate) services together are responsible for 58.6 per cent of contraceptive outlays (15.6 and 43 per cent respectively), the remaining 42.4 per cent being controlled by the private sector. The mix of methods is balanced, with female sterilization rates reaching 18.3 per cent but lagging far behind the use of reversible methods (44.2 per cent of women in a relationship).[26]

In Brazil, the public sector is responsible for 28.3 per cent of outlays; 3.4 per cent of services are managed by the non-governmental system (mainly Bemfam, the national IPPF associate) and 68.3 per cent are in the hands of the private sector. Long-standing state inaction with regard to Brazilian women's reproductive needs was replaced by the invisible hands of the market, which gradually dominated the supply of contraceptives. Although marginal in terms of services provided, the impact of the non-government family planning system has not been innocuous. The programmes have exposed poor women to modern contraception, but the lack of adequate information and the poor quality of services resulted in women's profound mistrust of reversible methods.

The contraceptive method mix in Brazil reflects that mistrust, as it is restricted to the pill and female sterilization (41 per cent and 44 per cent of contraceptive users in 1986). More than 80 per cent of pill users are supplied by drugstores. In 1986, 58.2 per cent of sterilizations were paid for privately, often as part of a caesarean section (Alencar and Andrade 1993). Brazilian caesarean section rates – among the highest in the world – are linked to the sky-rocketing rates of sterilization (Berquó 1993b). Beyond its association with class and race discrimination, sterilization in Brazil is emblematic of how market forces function in response to contraceptive needs. For millions of women recourse to sterilization has been a desperate way out from poverty, gender constraints and the absolute lack of enabling conditions favouring reproductive choice (Corrêa and Petchesky 1994).

In the Republic of Korea, a distinct model of combined policies has evolved. The Korean government has invested heavily in family planning since the 1970s, through both the public sector and non-governmental services. But Cho (1993a) argues that Korea's drop in fertility (67.6 per cent) must be viewed in the context of rapid economic growth and women's entry into the paid labour force. In another article (1993b), the author analyses the Korean fertility transition, identifying negative aspects that coincide with some of the structural features of Colombia and Brazil:

> Several studies point to a reluctance by men to co-operate with their partners in contraception ... The rate of induced abortion has increased rather than decreased, in spite of the fact that abortion is not legal except for medical reasons ... The rate of hysterectomies is extremely high.

In Korea, a small number of couples use vasectomy (11 per cent) and condoms (10 per cent), while in Brazil and Colombia the prevalence of male methods is even more limited: one per cent for vasectomies and 2 per cent for condoms in Brazil and less than one per cent (vasectomies) and 3 per cent (condoms) among Colombian men (Ross et al. 1993). Incidence of abortion is another area of commonality. Petchesky (1990), among others, suggests that when fertility regulation is integrated in women's lives, abortion becomes a necessary back-up resource. Korea now disputes the world record with Poland for the greatest number of abortions, and Brazilian abortion rates are also among the highest in Latin America.[27] In the three countries, although procedures are easily available, abortion remains illegal, with Colombia's legislation most restrictive.

Throughout Latin America, health risks related to clandestine abortion primarily affect poor women. In Brazil, of every 100 women who have induced abortions, 42 per cent suffer some kind of complication. In Colombia, this decreases to 29 per cent (Alan Guttmacher Institute 1994).[28] Although abortion is not registered as a major public health problem in Korea, Cho (1993b) hypothesizes that high rates of hysterectomies there could be related to myomata resulting from repeated abortion procedures. Both the increasing incidence of hysterectomies in Korea and Brazil's high prevalence of caesarean sections are consequences of the highly medicalized 'reproductive management' model prevailing in those countries.

Many dimensions of the Brazilian, Colombian and Korean experiences could be interpreted as results of the countries' economic development; they also convincingly demonstrate that development is not always the best contraceptive. While the demographic outcomes of their fertility management strategies have been extremely successful, women's overall health conditions have worsened, and the programmes failed to challenge gender inequalities or provide enabling conditions favouring women's reproductive self-determination.[29]

Pro-natalism

Pro-natalism is grounded in cultural and religious values, but – as historical experience in both the South and the North demonstrate – it is also related to economic development. In contrast to explicit government fertility control measures, pro-natalism is more frequently implicit in cultural values or nationalist ideologies than legislated by government. But the effects of persuading or forcing women to have more children than they desire may be as harmful to women as abuses committed in the name of population control. Ross et al. (1993) identified ten governments that do have explicitly designed population growth strategies: Gabon, Iraq, Kuwait, Oman,

Saudi Arabia, Cambodia, Korean Democratic Republic, Laos, Singapore, Taiwan and Uruguay.[30] DAWN has identified still other countries where pro-natalist ideologies have, to different degrees, influenced demographic policies: Chile, Argentina, Nicaragua and Guyana.

In the case of Chile, pro-natalism has never been explicit, but the Pinochet dictatorship (1973–90) reinforced traditional conservative biases against reproductive self-determination. Even the legal provision permitting abortion if the mother's life was at risk was suppressed on the eve of Chile's democratization in 1990 and has not been re-established (Matamala 1993). Yet Chile has the second highest abortion rate in a sample of six countries surveyed by the Alan Guttmacher Institute (1994).[31]

In Argentina, the military dictatorship of the 1970s imposed strict restrictions on the dissemination of contraceptives. While the restrictive regulations have now been suspended, the Catholic Church's powerful influence on government policies, partiularly in the mid-1980s, blocked reforms in abortion legislation (Bianco 1993). And the Vatican continues to play a clear role in Argentina's policy, strongly influencing the country to assume an anti-abortion position during the ICPD preparatory process.[32]

Nicaragua is often cited as a case where population control interventions have been relatively active (Dixon-Mueller 1993; Ross et al. 1993). But Pizarro (1993) describes an entirely different picture: in the 1980s, 'in a country characterized by rural production and mono-culture, an economic model was established that required many arms to work'. The economic growth model did not recognize the interrelation between production and reproduction. Women were expected to produce children as labourers and to replace the human losses from the liberation and ensuing war. Now, in the 1990s, the Chamorro government praises 'the universal value of the family, the return to the household and domestic activities'. In the wake of the war, this renewed pro-natalist ideology is dispensed to heal the country's wounds and solve Nicaragua's profound economic and social crisis.

Haniff's (1993) investigation of poor women's experiences with abortion in Guyana concludes that the country's high incidence of abortion there is related to a range of factors – among them, official pro-natalism.[33] Guyana's population has fallen as a result of economic crisis, eroded livelihoods and consequent out-migration (see also Wiltshire 1992). To counteract this trend, the government restricted access to family planning during the 1980s. For many women, abortion then became a primary means of fertility regulation. (More recently, limited contraceptive assistance services have been restored.) Women who sought abortions most frequently cited economic pressure as their primary reason for terminating pregnancy. But Haniff identified other, less explicit, motivations, including negative experiences with contraceptive methods and the absence of male collaboration in contraception and childrearing. The author found that women who opt for abortion may be expressing a form of resistance to the economic model, pro-natalist ideology, gender systems and lack of contraceptive options. In this sense, the Guyanese experience is not unusual. Historically, many women have refused to reproduce when treated as mere incubators.[34]

DOUBLE-STANDARD POLICIES: A RE-EMERGING TREND? The manipulation of demographic policies to target certain subaltern groups has been with us at least since the inception of eugenic thought in the nineteenth century. Although strains of the double-standard approach are present all over the world, the most blatant contemporary case was South Africa under apartheid. The South African government promoted the increase of the white population by providing tax incentives for larger white families and encouraging white immigration. At the same time, fertility control policies were implemented to reduce the black population. Under apartheid, women factory workers were threatened with losing their jobs unless they submitted to contraceptive injections; Soweto schoolgirls were denied the right to sit for matriculation examinations unless they had contraceptive injections, and there were many accounts of sterilization and fitting of IUDs for women without their knowledge (Brown 1987;

Klugman 1990). Klugman (1991) analysed the South African logic as follows:

> The national population program is the means through which the government seeks to ensure the decline of the population growth rate, especially among the 'least developed' members of the population – Africans ... The motivations for the population program are implicitly political, ensuring the maintenance of wealth and access to resources in the hands of a small minority and at the expense of the population as a whole. The program is premised on the concept of population groups and the maintenance of the inequalities between them.[35]

A significant insight to emerge from the DAWN debates was that many other governments appear to be fashioning population policies that reflect internal ethnic, racial or tribal cleavages. In Cameroon, for example, tribal and regional divisions of power could easily lead to official double-standard policies: fertility control would be promoted in the west and pro-natalism would prevail in the south. A similar pattern could evolve out of the regional tensions in Nigeria described by Madunagu (1994). In the Asian regional meeting, participants pointed to religious fundamentalism and ethnic discrimination as factors underlying state discourse on demographic policies. In India, fertility differentials between Hindus and the Islamic populations could constitute an explosive ingredient in aggravating ethnic strife.

Singapore and Malaysia's policies already clearly incorporate double standards. In Singapore, employment and social security benefits are provided as incentives to fertility among the well-off, particularly ethnic Chinese (Mukherjee 1993). In Malaysia, pronatalist measures reinforce national 'development' and Islamic state religion dominated by the country's ethnic Malays. Through a series of official incentives, Muslims are encouraged to have more children than the ethnic Chinese and Indians (Abdullah 1993). Singapore's policy had measurable impacts – fertility has increased by 3.5 per cent over the past decade. But in Malaysia, fertility decline projected for the the 1990–95 period is greater (9.5 per cent) than it was in the previous decade (Ross et al. 1993).[36]

In the Pacific region, where ethnic diversity is extremely accentuated, Dr Roberta Sykes (personal communication) reports massive sterilization campaigns against aboriginal women in the Northern Territory of Australia in the 1970s, and Griffen (1993) reports a similar trend against Indo-Fijians in Fiji and indigenous women in Kanaky (New Caledonia):

> Population programmes have focused on ethnic differences between indigenous Fijians and Indo-Fijians. Fertility control interventions have targeted Indo-Fijians; in the French colony of Kanaky (New Caledonia), the independence movement has been concerned over a French-supported settler policy that is directed at making the indigenous Kanaks a minority.

These experiences, while shocking because they are little-known beyond their borders, reflect practices that have a long history. In the United States, as recently as the 1990s, Norplant has been meted out as a punishment to poor African-American women, particularly women who have AIDS or who face criminal charges such as drug use or child abuse. This official manipulation of women's health status or crime record to justify yet another form of population control has created a backlash growth in the number of African-American reproductive rights activists. African-American women have organized renewed efforts to monitor contraceptive development and approval procedures, to challenge population control policies domestically and overseas, and to educate large numbers of African-American women about reproductive rights. The emerging African-American analysis of reproductive rights will force the reproductive rights movement to become more relevant to the ongoing struggle against racism and poverty in the USA (Ross 1993).

Native American women in the USA have also mobilized politically to combat massive sterilization of indigenous women. The government Indian Health Service is reported to have encouraged high rates of sterilization among young women, and many clinics have dubious records of having procured informed consent. Many women were given the impression that they would lose their welfare benefits if they didn't submit to a tubal ligation. When these reports

Box 1.2 Threats to the basic needs approach

Some experiences with fertility regulation have avoided the distortions that prevail in most of the world. Programmes following 'basic needs' development premises have supported fertility management without inflicting enormous costs to woman's health, rights and general well being. Sri Lanka and Cuba, the Indian state of Kerala and, to a lesser extent, Costa Rica fit this description.

In Sri Lanka, investment in family planning is a government priority within broader concerns for universal education and primary health care. Sri Lankan services distinguish themselves from the poor-quality, coercive services prevalent in most of South Asia, and its drop in fertility (51.9 per cent) surpasses that of all its neighbouring countries. The policy has not been perfect, however. By feminist standards, sterilization rates are too high: 30 per cent in 1987, with 5 per cent corresponding to male vasectomy.

Structural adjustment began in the late 1970s, and during the 1980s targeted poverty-oriented programmes replaced the previously universal schemes. Subsequent increased poverty resulted in female out-migration and disruptions in reproductive patterns.

In Cuba, fertility was already declining at the time of the 1959 Revolution. With the Revolution, women's political and legal status improved, family planning was integrated into a universal basic health programme and abortion was legalized. By implementing those reforms, Cuba broke away from oppressive religious and ideological values prevailing in Latin America. Since the 1970s, Cuba has received international donor support without compromising its principles, but more recently both its comprehensive health and abortion policies have been threatened by economic and political pressures.

Instead of following conventional economic guidelines, Cuba has defined this as a 'special period of adjustment'; in contrast to structural adjustment, the Cuban government continues to emphasize equitable distribution of scarce resources. Health and education programmes have been strengthened. Financial resources have diminished, but the community-based preventive health system is still in place and access to contraception and safe abortion is unaffected (information summarized from Cutié Cancino (1993a, 1993b) and Perera (1993)).

became public, a Federal government investigation was initiated by a Congressional inquiry. A US Congressional aide remarked: 'You don't have to have a conspiracy to have the effect of one. The attitudes of racism and sexism have been translated into an excess of sterilizations. I would call it genocide' (Louv, no date).

Reshaping policies: political challenges

Fertility management policies have had undeniable negative effects on women's health and well-being around the world. In addition to coercion by population programmes, discrimination and poor services, data on contraceptive prevalence, maternal mortality and unsafe abortion provide empirical evidence of persistent gender biases in programme implementation (Berquó 1993a; Dixon-Mueller 1993; Ross et al. 1993; Sundstrom 1993; Alan Guttmacher Institute, 1994). Southern women are subject to second-class standards, whether as subjects of fertility control or of pro-natalist policies.

But the history of the last three decades does not portray a linear evolution of demographic policies. The 1984 shift in population policy at the Mexico Conference illustrates how even macro-level definitions have not been continous. Instability has charaterized regional and national policies as well. For example, Batliwala (1993) demonstrates how India's population policy from the 1950s to the 1990s moved from a 'soft' cafeteria approach to a developmentalist 'basic needs' perspective and then to the vasectomy 'camp' strategy. Domestic reactions and international human rights critiques of the camps prompted a return to targeting women's fertility, which remains in place today. As another example, African governments historically resisted population policies, but under the pressures of structural adjustment in the 1980s, they established official population policies. Marcelo (1993) portrays a similar contradictory pattern in the Philippines' political process. With the democratic struggle against dictatorship and imperialism, the state's previous heavy-handed fertility control policy was only to be replaced by an official pro-natalist position (see also Dixon-Mueller 1993). Today, policies in the Philippines are taking yet another direction.[37] Finally,

in Latin America both neo-Malthusians and pro-natalists have historically obstructed women's self-determination.

In the logic of dominant powers, shifts from population control
to strategies that view women as incubators (and vice-versa) are not
as radical as they may appear. Even when policies maintain a consistent set of goals, the design and scope of interventions may change
over time. Recognizing this instability allows us to deconstruct the
notion that policies are immutable – a perception that has frequently
paralysed feminist discourse about reform of existing policy definitions. If population policies can change in one direction, they can
switch again, subject to political forces. The politics of 'fertility
management' run from macro-policies to the ground level, where
resistances are spawned and mature. All the links of the chain are
critical points of entry for political intervention. Consequently, feminists must explore many political terrains and influence them with
our analyses and actions.

Policies at the national and international level are subject to
transformation whenever social relations and cultural norms are
challenged from the ground. Our task is to sustain women's struggles
to restructure and 'engender' household dynamics while simultaneously confronting the social and political environments that
reinforce oppressive gender systems. The women's movement does
not operate in a vacuum but in permanent dialogue (and, sometimes,
conflict) with the other actors and voices that emerge and evolve
within civil society, including the powerful and contradictory non-
governmental family planning system.[38] And, since policies are defined by governments, we cannot avoid engaging with state systems to
challenge their postulates. This terrain is a minefield, as state-led
policies have historically meant abuse of women's rights (Kannabiran
1988). But the Southern feminist movement cannot evade involvement with states if we are to see the implementation of gender-
sensitive programmes, universal services and legal reforms.

At this point in history, state systems are experiencing turbulent
change. On the one hand, market forces have been unleashed to
shrink the state, while on the other, conservative fundamentalist

forces struggle for state control. Individual national governments no longer manage what has always been understood as 'state' apparatus, as emergent global economic, legal and political systems begin to appropriate many of their functions. The Bretton Woods institutions (including the World Bank, the International Monetary Fund, and the World Trade Organization, formerly the General Agreement on Tariffs and Trade) have gained enormous power in recent years, and the United Nations system is being reformed in order to cope with the challenges of the new world order. As international systems tend to globalize, most Southern governments are decentralizing. Therefore, our interaction with state systems will involve defining strategies to pressure and negotiate at local, national and global levels in this complex and fluid world order.[39]

Southern women have already accumulated a great deal of knowledge about state population policies. The challenge of the 1990s will be further to investigate how the expansion of market forces in the health sector and family planning programmes affect women's reproductive health and rights. We cannot abandon our political strategies to reverse market-oriented development paradigms, but our critical research and analyses should also provide proposals for monitoring and ensuring the quality and accountability of public and private programmes. Given the scope, complexity and instability of today's fertility management systems, the time frame for the transformations we seek is necessarily long-term. Drawing upon the experience of Southern feminists' efforts to reshape national policies during the last decade (García-Moreno and Claro 1994; Corrêa 1991; Dixon-Mueller 1993), we have learned that changes at the ground level are slow, and our effectiveness will depend on thoughtful and sustained political action.

Notes

1. In Ancient Rome, particularly after the Emperor Augustus, a series of laws conditioned transmission of property among patricians to civil marriage and procreation. Male Roman citizens could not inherit property from their fathers if they were living in concubinate or did not have a certain number of live children. Rousselle (1980) analyses how this state

regulation had a direct impact on medical practices and discourse about sexuality, reproductive behaviour and women's bodies.

2. As we know, in the case of Germany and, to a lesser extent in Japan, strict family rules applying to 'superior' groups were combined with brutal practices to eliminate those considered inferior. And between 1933 and the end of the Second World War 200,000 people were sterilized in Germany.

3. In Brazil, among various indirect policies, wage complements were provided for each newborn child (the 'family salary'). The policy is still in place but has lost economic value. All over Latin America, feminists have explored how the maternal-child health programmes implemented in the 1970s have interacted with pro-natalism to reinforce women's roles as 'reproducers' rather than citizens (Corrêa 1991).

4. Cabrera describes the following: 'As an aftermath of this congress, the booklet "Birth Regulation" was published and disseminated with remarkable success. It was written by the American nurse Margaret Sanger, initiator in several countries of the birth control movement. Additionally, in 1925, during the regime of a deeply anti-clerical president Calles, Ms Sanger's booklet was freely distributed throughout Mexico and three clinics were opened for the attention of women who wished to control their fertility.'

5. In the US, 'compulsory sterilization laws were common in the majority of states ... As many as 45,000 people in the US were sterilized between 1907 and 1945, and many of them were poor' (Ferringa et al. 1992). In 1942, the American Birth Control League, under the leadership of Margaret Sanger, changed its name to the Federation of Planned Parenthood, and shortly thereafter the International Planned Parenthood Federation (IPPF) was created. Significantly, the new organization initially shared a London Office with the British Eugenic Society (see Greer 1984).

6. In Bhawan's description: 'Birth control was advocated by some medical writers, and in 1928, with the support of many influential persons, including High Court judges, a neo-Malthusian league was formed in Madras City. In 1923, Professor R.D. Karve opened the first family planning clinic in Poona. Thanks to its enlightened prime minister, the native state of Mysore had opened the first government clinic in Bangalore in 1930 (although it attracted few clients). A society for the Study and Promotion of Family Hygiene was formed in Bombay in 1935, and the All-India Women's Conference also advocated the adoption of voluntary birth control. The impact of these efforts was limited to a very small section of the population, but private interest in spreading family limitation culminated in the formation of the Family Planning Association of India (FPAI) in 1949.'

7. Aside from the theoretical debate between the population control movement and developmentalists, progressive analysts considered the new theories to be more ideological than scientific. Given the geo-political atmosphere of the period in which they were popularized, particularly in the USA, the theories were viewed as a strategy to prevent the spread of communism in poor countries.

8. In India, the aftermath of Bucharest was the 'most historically significant period in the Indian population control program, thanks to serious human rights abuses committed in the name of family planning during the Emergency' (Batliwala 1993). China followed the same trend; in 1979 the Chinese Minister of Family Planning referred to the 'detrimental consequences of population growth to capital accumulation ... for the improvement in the standard of living and for overcoming shortages in industry' (in Mertens 1993).

9. The Mexico Conference keynote speech by the Brazilian Health Minister (Dr Waldir Arcoverde, 1980/1985), is poignant. In 1984, the Brazilian Government – a dictatorship in the process of democratization – had just approved a Women's National Health Programme, which included for the first time the provision of contraception within the public health system. The programme was informed and supported by the women's movement. But in the international scenario, the 1984 Brazilian position could be interpreted simply as the final surrender of a government well known for its resistance to implementing any type of fertility management policy.

10. The famous Ehrlich equation is written as $I = P \times T \times C$, where 'I' refers to the environmental impact, 'P' is the population factor, 'T' a technological factor and 'C' the level of consumption. The equation has been applied to evaluate the impact of population growth on circumstances as varied as deforestation, fertilizer use and numbers of motor vehicles. Amalric and Banuri (1993) critique the equation: '[it is] an apparently elegant way to measure the contribution of population growth to the global environmental crisis ... Written as it is, it is simply wrong unless we assume that consumption and technological factors are homogeneous across the entire population considered.'

11. During the 1992 UNCED process in Rio, the population establishment built an alliance with mainstream environmentalists as a lobbying strategy. The political atmosphere of the early nineties stimulated, within USAID for instance, the formulation of the so-called BIG programme targeting the most populated countries in the world (India, Brazil, Mexico, Nigeria and Indonesia among others) to become population control priorities in the 1990s. Advertisement of the programme coincided with preparations

for the conference, infuriating feminists and causing extremely detrimental effects on the ambience of the meeting.

12. Some countries are missing from the list: Belize, Guyana, Surinam, French Guyana; Barbados and a row of other Caribbean island states and the French colonies; in the Pacific, the list is restricted to Australia, New Zealand and Papua New Guinea. In Africa the two examples where no policies exist are Libya and Gabon. The majority of countries where no official family planning is implemented is concentrated in the Gulf area: Iraq, Kuwait, United Arab Emirates, Oman and Saudi Arabia. The Asian list includes Cambodia, Laos and Mongolia. In the case of Latin America, Bolivia is the exception. In three cases (Hong Kong, Taiwan and Puerto Rico), no clear reference is made to state-led policies.

13. While the classification system is more highly differentiated than previous data (Dixon-Mueller 1993), it still fails to distinguish among more nuanced characteristics of national policies, such as intensity of 'incentives' for service providers and acceptors, for example. The survey scores family planning programmes as 'strong' in China, Republic of Korea, Taiwan, Thailand, Sri Lanka, Indonesia, Mexico, Botswana, Bangladesh and India. The 'very weak or non-existent' category applies to seventeen countries. Nine of those coincide with Dixon-Mueller's typology: Libya, Gabon, Iraq, Kuwait, Oman, Saudi Arabia, United Arab Emirates, Cambodia and Laos. (Mongolia and Bolivia are not included.) The eight remaining 'very weak' policies (in Ross et al. 1993) are Sudan, Chad, Malawi, Côte d'Ivoire, Myanmar, Namibia and Liberia.

14. Data were collected between 1987 and 1992 from fourteen countries in Africa, nineteen in Latin America, four in the Middle East and thirteen in Asia. The countries are Mauritius, Nigeria (one state), Brazil, Colombia, Guyana, Mexico, Paraguay, Puerto Rico, Venezuela, Turkey, Malaysia and Pakistan. Data collected by feminist researchers suggest, however, that this information may not be accurate in all cases (Ávila 1989, for Brazil; Haniff 1993, for Guyana; Siddiqi 1993, for Pakistan).

15. The new text reads as follows: 'It has been estimated that in the developing countries and countries with economies in transition, the implementation of programmes in the area of [reproductive health, including those related to family planning], maternal health and the prevention of sexually transmitted diseases, as well as other basic actions for collecting and analyzing population data, will cost: [$17.0 billion in 2000, $18.5 billion in 2005, $20.5 billion in 2010 and $21.7 billion in 2015]. Of this, approximately 65 per cent is for the delivery system. Programme costs in the closely related components which should be integrated into basic national programmes for population and reproductive health are estimated as follows:

(a) The family planning component is estimated to cost: [$10.2 billion in 2000, $11.5 billion in 2005, $12.6 billion in 2010 and $13.8 billion in 2015]. This estimate is based on census and survey data which help to project the number of couples and individuals who are likely to be using family planning information and services. Projections of future costs allow for improvements in quality of care. While improved quality of care will increase costs per user to some degree, these increases are likely to be offset by declining costs per user as both prevalence and programme efficiency increase.

(b) The [reproductive health] component [(not including the delivery-system costs, which are summarized under the [family planning] component)] is estimated to [add/cost:] [$5.0 billion in 2000, $5.4 billion in 2005, $5.7 billion in 2010 and $6.1 billion in 2015]. The estimate for reproductive health is a global total, based on experience with maternal health programmes in countries at different levels of development, selectively including other reproductive health services. The full maternal and child health impact of these interventions will depend on the provision of tertiary and emergency care, the costs of which should be met by overall health sector budgets.

(c) The sexually transmitted disease/HIV/AIDS prevention programme is estimated by the WHO Global Programme on AIDS to cost: $1.3 billion in 2000, $1.4 billion in 2005 and approximately $1.5 billion in 2010 and $1.5 billion in 2015.' (United Nations 1994 'Draft Final Document of the Conference', 13 May, disseminated by the electronic conference ICPD. General/NGONET).

16. The case of Norplant abuse in the USA is probably the best illustration. See Forte (1994) and Scott (1992a).

17. In evaluating the Indonesian family planning programme, the World Bank (World Bank 1988) discarded the government proposition to gradually privatize existing services. The Bank's advocacy of subsidies for the sector openly contradicted its own macro-economic rules. The Bank argued that the efficacy of the Indonesian family planning programme would permit it to spare huge investments in creating employment and financing social programmes.

18. Mintzes et al. (1993), Raharjo (1993) and Ward et al. (1990) also discuss problems with Indonesia's National Family Programme.

19. The quota system led to: 'unimaginable atrocities committed on the poor, particularly the tribals, backward castes and minorities, to force them to undergo sterilization. Government employees faced salary cuts; children were barred from school if their parents were not sterilized; irrigation water was withheld from villages that did not fill their sterilization quotas' (Batliwala 1993).

20. Ross et al. (1993, Table 11) identify fifty-five programmes considered 'weak' and 'very weak' and about 50 per cent of those classified as 'moderate' could be also included under the 'incomplete' category.

21. Stable rates were identified in Ivory Coast, Mauritania, Niger, Madagascar, Somalia, Angola, Cameroon and Togo. Fertility is increasing in Guinea Bissau, Mali, Burkina Faso, Liberia, Sierra Leone, Burundi, Malawi, Uganda, Zambia, Tanzania, Ethiopia, Rwanda, Gabon, Zaire and Lesotho, with figures ranging from 1.25 per cent increases in Rwanda to 20.6 per cent in Burundi for the 1970–90 period (Dixon-Mueller 1993).

22. In 1987, two important events in Africa focused on reproductive health and fertility management. The Safe Motherhood Conference (February) and Better Health for Women and Children through Family Planning Conference (October, involving WHO, the World Bank, IPPF and UNFPA). In the latter case, arguments were raised to convince African governments of the need to integrate family planning in primary health programmes. Various papers presented at the conference relied on field data to prove that 'birth spacing' (meaning the use of contraception) prevented both infant and maternal mortality (Corrêa, unpublished manuscript).

23. Between 1970 and 1990 drops in fertility were 25.3 per cent in Zimbabwe, 17.2 in Kenya, 28.9 in Botswana 12.6 per cent in Nigeria; in the latter cases, the range was from 1.7 per cent in Central African Republic to 7.35 in Senegal (Dixon-Mueller 1993).

24. The DAWN debates in Nairobi explored important aspects of women's reproductive aspirations. If a new reproductive pattern is to emerge in Africa, it will take the form of child-spacing or a model of three children per woman, but never fewer than that. Moreover, preference for sons is still a strong influence in many settings, and a three-child model may easily extend to four, five or six, if a son does not appear.

25. The authors cite Judith Bruce's data: 'Men remain fertile longer than women and continue to have sexual activity into their older years. As a result, evidence from some countries shows that many men have higher fertility than their wives, and much of this occurs after age 45.'

26. 16.2 per cent of women in a relationship rely on the pill, 11 per cent use the IUD, 2.4 per cent use injectables, 2.3 use barrier methods and 12.3 use behavioural methods.

27. A recent study performed by the Alan Guttmacher Institute (1994) in Latin America provides the following information: in 1991, 1.4 million induced abortions were performed in Brazil, or 44 for every 100 live births; in Colombia, abortions are estimated to have reached 228,000 in the same year, or 35 for every 100 live births.

28. Although abortion legislation in Colombia is extremely restrictive, a

range of private and non-governmental reproductive health services have provided access to safe abortion since the 1980s.

29. Thailand's combined policy is similar to that of Korea (see Pyne 1994).

30. It is interesting to note that these are roughly the same countries where no fertility control interventions are being implemented (the exceptions being Taiwan and Singapore).

31. See Frasca's (1994) exploration of the pervasive effects of implicit biases about sexuality, adolescent fertility and abortion in Chile.

32. The Argentine delegation supported the Vatican's position during the ICPD Prepcom III negotiations.

33. Other factors cited are poor family planning services, inequitable gender relations and increasing poverty.

34. One example may be drawn from the experience of induced abortion among female slaves in the Americas who refused to reproduce for the slaveowners. Contemporary attempts to establish strict pro-natalist policies have faced similar resistance. In Ceausescu's Romania, women risked unsafe abortions rather than submitting to pro-natalist guidelines. Maternal mortality rates skyrocketed and when the regime fell, legal and safe abortions were prioritized. Nagaoki (1993) explores why Japanese women will not be easily persuaded by the recent government shift towards incentives favouring population growth.

35. Saman (no date) assesses the issue within the current context of democratization. Klugman (personnal communication 1994) describes the difficulty of maintaining women's reproductive self-determination on the political agenda without touching off sensitivities remaining from past double-standard policies.

36. This trend reflects the fact that the population targeted for pro-natalist policies (Malay) represents approximately 35 per cent of the Malaysian population. The remaining ethnic groups are subject to population control pressures.

37. In the Second Session of the ICPD Preparatory Commitee (in May 1993), the Philippines government strictly followed the Vatican's orientation. In the Third Session (in April 1994), NGOs were represented in the official Philippine delegation and the position shifted to support the reproductive health and rights framework.

38. The IPPF's strategic importance must be considered in at least two ways. Its past contributions to policy definition and programme implementation clearly fed on the neo-Malthusian fears of elites worldwide and must be forcefully challenged. However, if feminists seriously intend to transform population policies, the IPPF network cannot be ignored. Coalitions among women family planning service providers and feminist organizations are

already a positive reality in parts of Africa and other Southern contexts. The Caribbean experience also inspires hope.

39. The policy framework described here, despite structural distortions, may be favourable to change, since most population policies have remained 'incomplete'.

Sexual and reproductive health and rights:
the southern feminist approach

What do Native women in North America have in common with
African Brazilian women? Both groups may be sterilized without
their informed consent. Do Black South African women and indigenous women in the French colony of New Caledonia share any
common experience? Both are targeted for intensive fertility control
campaigns designed to shrink ethnic groups spurned by governments.

Historically, states and political movements all over the world
have attempted to manipulate women's lives, sexuality and fertility
for political purposes, whether in the guise of population control or,
more recently, fundamentalist revivals. For example, in 1984 in
Egypt, women lost the right to stay in the matrimonial home after
divorce or repudiation (a husband's rejection of his wife on the
basis of her childlessness, suspected adultery, or otherwise failing to
fulfil her marital duties) – a right they had struggled for over a
decade to gain. In 1989, Algerian men were delegated the right to
vote on behalf of their women relatives. In Pakistan, women are still
struggling against ordinances that condemn 'adulteresses' to death
by stoning or a hundred lashes.[1] As recently as 1990, Iraq passed a
decree allowing men to kill their womenfolk for adultery (Hélie-
Lucas 1993). And all over North America, Christian fundamentalists
have aggressively intimidated doctors and law-makers in an effort to
deny women access to legal abortion.

Women have responded to these and other resurgences of gender
violence by building an internationally recognized legal framework
for the universal defence of women's autonomy, bodily integrity and
personhood. The framework identifies how human rights instruments may be interpreted to condemn abuses of women's rights. It

also proposes modifications in existing legal tools and social policies. With explicit provisions protecting women's right to bodily integrity, the framework is a key instrument for guaranteeing that population programmes respect women. The framers of the strategy are now networking to mobilize women politically all over the world to protect the newly interpreted rights.

DAWN has interpreted and expanded the framework to more fully reflect Southern women's concerns (see Box 2.1).

Evolution of the framework
The United Nations women's decade
Drawing directly upon the West's historical concern for individual rights, the notion of universal human rights was first ratified in the United Nations Charter of 1945. The UN Universal Declaration of Human Rights in 1948 affirmed equality among sexes as a basic principle, but only in 1975 was women's condition seriously examined by an international body, when the United Nations sponsored meetings launching the Women's Decade; the 1975 International Women's Year Conference in Mexico City initiated the decade-long process that culminated in Nairobi in 1985.

Feminist criticisms of fertility control policies had been maturing throughout the 1970s, and at the 1975 International Women's Year Conference in Mexico women denounced coercive practices in contraceptive research and services (such as forced sterilization and incentives for contraceptive 'acceptors') as human rights abuses. Perhaps more importantly, women's activists were instrumental in ensuring that the 1975 Women's Conference 'grounded its assertion of the right to reproductive choice on a notion of bodily integrity and control', as follows:

It should be one of the principal aims of social education to teach the respect for physical integrity and its rightful place in human life. The human body, whether that of women or men, is inviolable and the respect for it is a fundamental element of human dignity and freedom (Freedman and Isaacs 1992).

Box 2.1 The DAWN reproductive health and rights framework

DAWN views reproductive health as inextricably intertwined with women's human rights. Therefore, DAWN's framework for women's reproductive rights and health incorporates attention to women's economically productive and cultural roles in addition to their biological reproductive functions. And in the biological context, DAWN's definition of reproductive health services includes not only access to contraceptive information and methods and legal abortion, but also STD and cancer prevention, prenatal care and mental health services, all within the context of comprehensive preventive health services. A further element of the DAWN perspective on reproductive health is respect for traditional health knowledge, much of which is gradually being destroyed by imposed medical technologies.

DAWN's comprehensive reproductive rights and health policy would guarantee women access to housing, education, employment, property rights and legal equality in all spheres. It would also secure women's freedom from physical abuse, harassment, genital mutilation and all forms of gender-based violence.

Our insistence upon a holistic analysis reveals DAWN's bias toward comprehensive health services as a key component of our proposal for social policies and infrastructure designed to meet people's (especially women's) basic needs. In Southern countries, we recognize an alarming trend away from state responsibility for basic needs, in which market forces have increasingly been employed to mobilize and distribute health resources that should be widely available to the public. Based on structural adjustment policies, this tendency toward privatizing the health sector isolates it from other basic services (which, in many cases, also are being privatized) and limits even further poor women's access to health care.

The key result of the UN Decade for Women was an international legal instrument, the Convention on the Elimination of all forms of Discrimination against Women (CEDAW), ratified in 1979. CEDAW was a major victory in the battle to secure women's equality with men, including the right to bodily integrity. However, CEDAW fails to specify a number of women's reproductive rights, except to affirm women's rights to family planning information, counselling and services and to have equal rights with men to decide on the number and spacing of their children.[2] In addition, CEDAW confirms women's rights to maintain their jobs while pregnant, to maternity leave and child care.

CEDAW obligates signatory states to modify discriminatory social and cultural patterns as well as their laws, in this way condemning customary rights based on religious doctrine, tradition or customs enforcing women's subordination.[3]

UN population conferences

Parallel to the women's decade and the consolidation of internationally recognized women's rights instruments, the UN held a series of international human rights and population conferences that also dealt directly with women's reproductive rights. The concept of universal rights was first applied to family planning twenty years after the Universal Declaration, at the 1968 International Human Rights Conference in Tehran: 'Couples have a basic human right to decide freely and responsibly on the number and spacing of their children and a right to adequate education and information in this respect.'[4]

In 1974, at the World Population Conference in Bucharest, Romania, the principle was slightly rephrased to extend the right to *individuals* (not just couples) and to indicate that people should have access to *means to exercise these rights*, a phrase that could be interpreted to cover a range of social and economic rights (Freedman and Isaacs 1993).[5] By 1984, although the Mexico debates were not closely monitored by the international women's movement, feminists present at the conference managed to ensure that women's issues received high visibility within the traditional framework of the resulting WPPA:

> Throughout the discussion of the World Population Plan of Action, female delegates from many countries – especially Australia and Zimbabwe – strengthened the language that emphasized the linkages between

high fertility and the lack of education, health care, and employment opportunities for women and their low status in general. Recommendations to overcome ... discrimination were moved from a later section of the plan on 'Reproduction, the family and status of women' to the front, following the section on socioeconomic development and population (Dixon-Mueller 1993).

These efforts were critical in counteracting the instrumental approach of enhancing women's status and promoting women's health, which was emerging in the discourse of the major population institutions (Dr Elza Berquó, personal communication). The final document stated that 'governments should make Family Planning widely available'. But, reflecting pressure applied by a conservative US administration and the Vatican, Mexico delegates also stressed that abortion was not to be considered a method of family planning.

The various UN conferences' resolutions on women's rights represented significant advances over the restricted civil and political human rights recognized by the previous UN Covenants. But population and family planning provisions were consistently oriented to birth control rather than an integrated approach to reproductive health, and their gender neutrality disregarded women's specific reproductive responsibility (see Petchesky and Wiener 1990). Finally, the UN resolutions utterly failed to address abortion rights.[6]

Among other critics, DAWN has questioned some of the terms of the international instruments. First, the language of the conference documents fails effectively to link women's rights to broader human rights principles (Boland, Rao and Zeidenstein 1994). Second, the documents demonstrate that women's central role in reproduction has never been an overriding concern of the population field.

Third, the private domain – including family relations, domestic violence, sexuality and reproduction – is considered to fall outside the purview of UN legislation. If democratic instruments are to serve as tools to reformulate the notion of citizenship, as Astelarra (1992) observes, they must recognize women's rights in the private domain, where power differentials are greatest.

Finally, feminists have identified a weakness in the core principles approved in 1968, 1974 and 1984 documents. In particular, their references to choosing family planning 'freely and responsibly' – which appear in all the statements – may be interpreted as culturally relative. As Freedman and Isaacs (1993) point out, this framing of the principles frustrates efforts to identify reproductive rights abuses in circumstances where coercion may not be explicit but results from cultural or political pressures.

The reproductive health and rights movement

At the time of the UN conferences (both the Women's Decade and the Population conferences), the concept of reproductive rights had not yet been formalized in feminist discourse. The ICASC - International Campaign on Abortion, Sterilization and Contraception, founded in Europe in 1978 to counter both pro-natalist and anti-natalist movements – may have been the first to formalize a concept that many women's organizations around the world had come to define as reproductive rights: 'women's right to decide whether, when and how to have children – regardless of nationality, class, race, age, religion, disability, sexuality or marital status – in the social, economic and political conditions that make such decisions possible.'[7]

In July 1984, just before the second World Population Conference took place in Mexico City, a large number of the world's women's health activists attended the first global conference convened by ICASC in Amsterdam. The Amsterdam Conference is often cited as the birth event of the International Reproductive Health and Rights Movement, bringing together individuals representing initiatives taken throughout the world. On that occasion the Campaign changed its name to Women's Global Network for Reproductive Rights (WGNRR), under pressure from Southern activists who felt that the explicit reference to reproductive rights would more appropriately encompass Southern women's health agenda (Ávila, personal communication). One underlying principle formed the basis for communication among the profusion of diverse women's groups: the belief that women should be seen as subjects and not objects of population policies.[8]

Until very recently, reproductive health initiatives evolved almost entirely independently of both the population establishment and 'women in development' networks. But feminists' diverse political strategies since 1984 finally culminated in the population establishment's recognition that family planning cannot be isolated from comprehensive health interventions.

Moreover, after three decades of intensive investment, the poor outcomes (in contraceptive prevalence, fertility decline and quality of services) of demographically oriented population policies had led some of the major actors in the field to reconsider their assumptions. Thus, by the end of the 1980s, the concept of reproductive health had been integrated into population discourse by mainstream institutions, such as in the Ford and MacArthur Foundations' Reproductive Health Programs, the 'quality of care' framework adopted by the Population Council and the World Bank's Reproductive Health recommendations (see World Bank 1993).[9]

Reproductive health: the emperor's new clothes?

Even after almost ten years of debate, not all of Southern women's concerns have been integrated by the mainstream reproductive health analysis. The mainstream's initial adoption of reproductive health discourse has largely maintained a biomedical bias and restricted women's social roles to their biological reproductive functions, especially by emphasizing maternal–child health and family planning programmes.[10] Hartmann (1993) expressed feminists' uneasiness by calling the new mainstream discourse the 'population double-speak'.[11] A speech by the Family Planning Director of Indonesia, Haryono Suyono, clearly illustrates why many feminists felt their ideas were being manipulated:

> The role of women has been given increasing importance as the main motivating factor behind the decision to limit fertility ... We have co-operated with other ministries to achieve an improvement in the role and status of women. A State Ministry for Women's Affairs was set up,

women's organizations were encouraged and given support to become involved in community welfare and other projects ... and other such approaches which in essence fall outside the family planning realm proper but can be harnessed for our purposes.[12]

Aside from the risk of potential manipulation, conceptual problems were embedded in the establishment's new discourse. The population institutions focused on micro-level dimensions: gender systems in the family,[13] sexuality, access to adequate health services and education programmes. While Southern women affirmed the critical importance of those dimensions, they called for an approach integrating the micro-dimensions with larger issues such the transformation of state social, demographic and economic development policies to incorporate women's social and economic rights. As in the Indonesian case, some states and institutions have subsequently extended their frameworks to include limited social and economic rights, as a means of improving women's status. Such measures, and in fact the 'women's status' approach as a whole, are interpreted by many feminists as an instrumental strategy to reduce fertility.

Political conditions determine the opportunities and limits of feminists' ability to negotiate with the powerful population institutions. In stable democratic societies, civic interest groups may be able to protect their autonomy from institutional interests. But in authoritarian or newly democratic settings, the vast power differentials among institutions and citizens' groups may limit the independence of civil society. Given the latter circumstances in much of the developing world, many activists have interpreted the reproductive health discourse of mainstream development institutions and governments as a manipulation of the feminist position in order to achieve the goal of fertility reduction.[14] For example, Bandarage found that

> Coalition building and alliances among different social change movements is essential for finding effective, long term solutions to the complex problems facing the world. Yet, it is important to bear in mind that ruling interests tend to confuse and co-opt social movements that challenge them by manipulating progressive terminologies, offering funds and other tactics. There are many historical precedents to the co-optation

of liberal feminist birth control struggles by population control interests, especially in the United States (Bandarage 1994).

Common ground: reproductive health and development

Despite the risks of manipulation, in DAWN's view women must apply pressure and negotiate with the development establishment (including the population community) to carve out our own political space. This is especially important because women's reproductive health must be placed within a comprehensive human development framework that promotes all people's well-being and women's full citizenship. Reframing the population field may be a partial yet critical step in integrating women's needs and rights into global development paradigms. Towards that end, we have identified specific points of intersection linking the reproductive health framework to current efforts to reframe development objectives:

— much of the reproductive health framework is drawn directly from a 'basic needs' agenda;

— the framework is consistent with the 'human development' approach;

— the framework calls for public investment to reach the poorest women, and provides for social and economic 'enabling conditions' necessary to women's exercise of their reproductive rights; and

— the framework identifies the public health system as a key mediator between individual women, households, social structures and the state.

The strongest common feature is an underlying conviction that meeting the basic needs of the world's poorest people, especially women, will empower them to gain control over their own lives and livelihoods, and is the most effective means of promoting equitable economic growth, human rights and sustainable development.

Box 2.2 Reproductive health and justice: International Women's Health Conference for Cairo '94

In January 1994, women from all over the world produced a declaration to be delivered to heads of state and drafters of the ICPD Programmeme of Action. Following are excerpts from the declaration:

'Inequitable development models and strategies constitute the underlying basis of growing poverty and marginalization of women, environmental degradation, growing numbers of migrants and refugees, and the rise of fundamentalism everywhere. For women these problems (and their presumed solutions through economic programmes for structural adjustment which promote export production at the expense of local needs and reduce the role of the state in the social sector) have particularly severe consequences.

'The situation of women migrants who are heads of households, domestic servants, migrant workers, entertainers and other service workers, and the brutality and violence faced by women and children who are victims of trafficking and sexual exploitation is of particular concern. The movement of people should not be constrained by discriminatory migration policies which operate in contexts where migration is forced by economic hardship, civil strife, war and political persecution.

'There is a need to design social development policies starting from the concerns and priorities of women. These include: redistribution of resources; restoration of basic services eroded by macro-economic policies; provision of comprehensive health services addressing the reproductive health needs of women and men of all ages; strengthening of women's participation in political and policy-making processes; building accountability mechanisms into policies.

'Fundamentalists use religion, culture and ethnicity in their pursuit of power. Such movements represent a new form of war against women and an aggressive attempt to mutilate their human rights.

'Reproductive health services should include not only safe contraception but also safe abortion and prevention, early diagnosis and treatment of sexually transmitted diseases including HIV/AIDS. The UN and other donors and governments should recognize the right to safe and legal abortion as an intrinsic part of women's rights, and governments should change legislation and implement policies to reflect such a recognition.

'Better health services are one element of women's rights. In addition, sexuality and gender power relationships must be addressed as a central aspect of reproductive rights.

'Reproductive rights are human rights which are inalienable and inseparable from basic rights such as the right to food, shelter, health, security, livelihood, education and political empowerment.

'Women are entitled to bodily integrity. Within this principle, violence against women and harmful practices like female genital mutilation must be recognized as a major reproductive rights and health issue. Governments should be held accountable for taking measures to combat such practices.

'Women should be involved in the decision making processes national and internationally where any laws or policies affecting their rights and health are designed and implemented.'

The indivisibility of health and rights

Women have exploited the common ground between feminists and the population and development communities to apply organized pressure – coordinated by a number of women's international networks – to articulate a clear feminist position within the ICPD process. At present, the Cairo document includes concerns for gender equality, the right to physical integrity, security of the person and reproductive rights. Throughout 1992 and 1993, DAWN, Women's Environment and Development Organization (WEDO), the Women's Global Network for Reproductive Rights (WGNRR) and the International Women's Health Coalition (IWHC), among others, organized a series of regional meetings and caucuses at the preparatory committees to articulate and coordinate women's input into the UN process. A key product of this process is the Declaration of the Reproductive Health and Justice International Conference, which was approved by 215 representatives from seventy-nine countries.

In preparation for the ICPD, women have engaged their country representatives in dialogue at local, regional and international levels,

---

Box 2.3 The ICPD Draft Programme of Action

The ICPD document defines reproductive health as physical, mental and social well-being (not just the absence of disease), and the ability to exercise one's human sexuality without health risks. Sexual health is defined as the integration of physical, emotional, intellectual and social aspects of sexual being, and the objective of sexual health services should be to encourage personal relationships and individual development, not just treatment of reproductive health problems and sexually transmitted diseases.

The document declares that sexual and reproductive rights include certain human rights that are already officially recognized: basic rights of individuals and couples to decide on the number and spacing of their children, and rights to information and accessible services to that end; the right to respect for security of the person and physical integrity of the human body; and the right to non-discrimination and freedom from violence (see Chapter VII on Reproductive Rights, Sexual and Reproductive Health and Family Planning).

---

resulting in an ICPD document that by the time of the April 1994 session of the preparatory committee incorporated most of women's concerns. The holistic perspective on sexual and reproductive health and rights that women have long struggled to promote now constitutes the conceptual framework that permeates the official ICPD Draft Programme of Action (see Box 2.3).

As a result of many years of women's determined organizing and lobbying internationally, the population field will never again be the same. However, a long road lies ahead, as the document still contains numerous brackets around language to be contested in Cairo. The Vatican has proven its intransigence throughout the preparatory process, reading 'abortion rights' into concepts in the document such as 'safe motherhood' and 'sexual and reproductive health'. Other key rights concepts in the document, such as 'equality', 'diversity', 'personhood' and 'bodily integrity' (see Corrêa and Petchesky 1994) will face resistance not only from the Vatican, but also from fundamentalists and sectors of the population establishment.

However, if the ICPD process overcomes those powerful resistances and the document is approved as it stands, it will actually represent Southern feminists' hard-won interests. Our next challenge will then be to organize women to support forcefully the document's *integrated approach to reproductive health and rights* at national levels. Each country setting will suggest which specific problems are priority issues for applying this political strategy, but it is critical to underline the importance of consistently and convincingly integrating health and rights dimensions at all levels of implementation. For example, abortion and AIDS are two striking cases of how rights and health are intertwined and must be addressed as a continuum.

Abortion: a rights and health issue

Women's subordination has forced many women to accept unwanted pregnancies, often along with unwanted marital and sexual relations. As we know, the costs of pregnancy and motherhood – emotionally, physically and materially – are high. Therefore, throughout history and around the world, women have resorted to abortion as a form of fertility regulation.

In many cultures, abortion – whether by herbs, uterine massage or other means – is an integral part of traditional fertility control practices to regulate the timing and number of births.[15] Among African slave communities, abortion was a means women used to resist the institution of slavery by not bringing their children into the world.

Now that safe means of terminating a pregnancy are available and legal in many countries, women may consider their alternatives and make ethical decisions based on their particular circumstances. Abortions are more common at the end of the childbearing period in traditional societies such as Tunisia, Egypt and India, while in Western Europe and the USA, abortion is more frequently used to postpone the birth of the first child.

A woman's decision to terminate a pregnancy is surrounded by factors that vary from one culture to another, but nearly always involve family economic or health considerations, or both. Women may or may not construe their decision as having anything to do with gender relations or 'rights'. Just the same, a woman's decision represents a balancing of her own, her family's, and sometimes her community's needs. This decision – whether taken alone or in dialogue with significant others – represents a critical marker of women's reproductive autonomy and her right to health.

As an issue emblematic of feminist battles on several fronts, the campaign for legal abortion may be considered to have inaugurated the contemporary feminist movement for reproductive rights and freedom. Abortion, at the centre of the movement's most heated debates, sparked a political process that transformed the Northern population field during the 1980s. Despite women's activism, the UN Conference documents are not explicit about abortion rights. When abortion is discussed, it is framed as an epidemiological problem, as Dixon-Mueller (1993) notes:

> Where abortion has been mentioned at all in the recommendations of major international conferences on maternal and child health, human rights, population, and the status of women, it has usually been in recognition of the need to reduce high levels of maternal morbidity and mortality associated with clandestine procedures. But with a few notable exceptions, participants have been reluctant to endorse publicly the legalization of abortion and the expansion of safe and accessible services as a solution.

A major turning point in the struggle for recognition of abortion rights internationally was the Christopher Tietze International Symposium on Women's Health in the Third World, held in Brazil in 1988. The symposium participants, made up of physicians, researchers, legal experts and feminists from all over the world, declared that 'safe, legal, and affordable services for terminating unwanted pregnancies should be available to women in all countries on health and human rights grounds.'[16]

Women's advocacy strategies for abortion rights have not been uniform within or across regions, but they have developed around two major axes in both the North and the South: the *health rationale*,

Box 2.4 The legal status of abortion

In spite of the fact that abortion has been widely practised for centuries, its legality has been subject to the tides of history. Before the nineteenth century, there is no evidence that early abortions were condemned or even regulated legally. But during the ninteenth century, women in colonialized nations and the colonizers in most of Europe and North America faced legal restrictions on abortion at any stage of pregnancy.

According to Sundstrom (1993), by 1954 abortion was illegal in practically all countries of the world except Iceland, Denmark, Sweden and Japan. Since that time, abortion on request or under certain conditions has become legal in twenty-three countries. Northern countries have tended to liberalize their abortion laws, with the notable exception of the USA.[17] Since the dissolution of the Soviet Union, progressive abortion codes in some Eastern European countries (Croatia, Germany) have come under pressure from the Catholic Church, and some countries have approved more restrictive laws. Cuba is the only Latin American country with free legal abortion services (Cutié Cancino 1993a).

Abortion is still strictly illegal in most African and Latin American countries,[18] while under specific medical or social conditions, a legal abortion may be obtained in India, Zambia and Uruguay, for example. But about one-third of all Southern women are denied access to any legal abortion. The world's most populous countries are among the twenty-three nations where abortion is not restricted: China, India, the former Soviet Union and the US. Governments in China and Vietnam promote abortion as a means to limit population growth.[19] But in some countries where abortion is legal, such as India and China, the services are inappropriate or inaccessible for the majority of women because governments are coercive or fail to provide adequate resources and trained personnel (Sundstrom 1993). In one study of an Indian government family planning programme, Jyotsna Gupta found that women with two children or more were denied an abortion unless they agreed to a sterilization procedure at the same time (Gupta 1993).

which denounces the illegality of abortion as a major contributing factor to women's mortality around the world; and the *rights ration-*

ale, which asserts that a woman's right to terminate a pregnancy is a fundamental and inalienable one protected by fundamental principles of individual human rights. The strategies are not mutually exclusive; they have been used simultaneously by feminists in many countries, sometimes targeting separate audiences.

The health rationale for legalizing abortion has prevailed in much of Africa and Asia since the 1980s. According to this perspective, the health risks of abortion result not from medical factors but from its illegality. Illegality, together with social biases and taboos restricting abortion to the realm of informal practitioners, has resulted in the high rates of maternal morbidity and mortality described above. The health rationale for legalizing abortion denounces such high rates of mortality, illness, disease and long-term consequences resulting from clandestine abortions as morally reprehensible. Applying a disease model of public health, the advocates of this approach cite the alarming rates of abortion as an epidemic that must be addressed as a health issue.

From a second public health angle, sepsis resulting from unsafe abortions represents an enormous cost to public health systems. Particularly in Southern countries, where resources for health are already scant, societies cannot afford to bear the costs of keeping abortion illegal. Sundstrom (1993) supports this argument:

> In the National Hospital in Kenya, for example, women with abortion-related complications are said to occupy about 60% of acute gynecological beds ... In developing countries treatment of abortion-related complications may consume as much as 50% of hospital budgets ... [which is] much more expensive than providing medically safe abortions.

Legalization of abortion on request without bureaucratic obstacles is undoubtedly a necessary condition for the provision of safe services to all women who need them. However, it is not sufficient. Even where abortion is partially or wholly legal, Southern countries lack facilities and trained technicians. In addition, passive opposition to abortion may take the form of restrictive hospital policies or the reluctance or refusal of some health professionals to perform abortions. All such factors, added to the lack of resources and social pressures to feel shame or guilt, may deter women who are legally eligible from obtaining safe services.

Even feminists who strongly support the rights rationale for advocating legal abortion recognize that the health rationale may be more compelling to a broad public. Alliances have been built with international maternal mortality and safe motherhood campaigns, gaining high visibility and legitimacy in recent years.

The rights approach to advocating legal abortion argues that, independently of the public health issues involved, women are entitled to control their own reproduction.[20] Advocates cite the basic right of couples to 'decide freely and responsibly on the number and spacing of their children' which has been established by UN documents since 1968 (the rights of *individuals* to choose was only established in 1974). In 1969, the UN recognized governments' corresponding obligation to provide families with the 'knowledge and means necessary to enable them to exercise this right'. Taken together, the provisions are considered to provide the international legal framework necessary to guarantee a woman's right to terminate a pregnancy (Corrêa and Petchesky 1994).

Another angle of legal argument has been the right to individual privacy, as applied in US Supreme Court abortion decisions. In the USA, the rationale for this argument has been that abortion is essentially a private medical decision, guaranteed by the US Constitution. While bodily integrity is also a strong cultural value in the USA, it is not as constitutionally inviolable as the privacy right. The rationale is strongly Western.

More research is needed to examine how a woman's right to make her own decisions regarding fertility and reproduction are construed in other cultural settings. If privacy and bodily integrity are not key strategic rationales, as they have come to be in the West, what would be an equally powerful rationale in an African or Asian context?[21]

Some progressive human rights scholars and activists argue a position entirely different from the privacy or bodily integrity rationales. They assert that human rights entitlements are not just morally defined in the abstract, but must be grounded in cultural, social and political conditions. This may have been the rationale of Sister Ivone Gebara, for example, who found that forcing poor women to provide for undesired children was untenable and unjust, given Brazil's rapacious social inequalities (Gebara 1994; Nanne and Bergamo 1993).

However, applying this rationale alone, independent of an absolute concept of individual rights, runs the risk of effecting a definition of rights that is mutable, subject to change as a consequence of historical developments. This line of reasoning, then, represents a slippery slope, as it may be applied to relativize *all* human rights demands/violations as culturally defined.

In a highly contested use of the concept of fundamental rights, opponents of legalization, including the Catholic Church, fundamentalists and other conservative forces, use the women's rights argument as a springboard. They claim that the embryo or foetus is also entitled to its human rights, especially the right to life. DAWN researchers from Africa report that these anti-abortion forces are well organized through the churches, both Catholic and Protestant, across the continent. But a straightforward argument against the 'human rights of the foetus' position is that there is neither a clear scientific nor theological determination that before viability, foetal life is human life.

In order to extend the struggle for abortion rights beyond the boundaries of the feminist movement, women must engage allies in dialogue to define advocacy strategies appropriate to diverse cultural and political contexts. In many settings the women's movement has opted to pursue the health rationale, viewing it as more morally compelling than the rights argument in their particular context. The two rationales should not be seen as opposing alternatives, but rather as lines of reasoning and argument that converge upon the same goal: women's access to safe, legal abortion.

HIV/AIDS: a rights and health issue

Initiated by feminists, the rights rationale has dominated the abortion debate since its beginning. Health rationales were drawn in only

Box 2.5 AIDS and the worldwide sex industry

The World Health Organization estimates that the number of AIDS cases worldwide reached 2.5 million by mid-1993 and that between 30 and 40 million people will have been infected with HIV by the end of the decade if prevention strategies don't improve. In 1993, about 80 per cent of all HIV infections occurred in developing countries, where the infection is transmitted mainly through heterosexual intercourse. Sex workers are a critical link in this spreading heterosexual pattern of transmission.

AIDS rates in Asia are highest among sex workers in India, Thailand and the Philippines. In Puerto Rico, AIDs is the leading cause of death among women aged 15 to 44, suggesting a similar pattern of heterosexual transmission. And in Africa, the greatest concentration of HIV-infected persons is among women with a history of sexually transmitted diseases. Initially, the epidemic in Africa affected mainly urban sex workers. By 1988, the virus had spread among all social strata and both rural and urban populations. Nevertheless, urban sex workers and their clients still have the highest seropositive rates. Poorer sex workers have higher rates. For example, in Kenya, 66 per cent of lower-class sex workers tested positive, versus 31 per cent of high-class sex workers (Mann et al. 1988).

at a later stage, as a tactic to gain broader bases of support. In contrast, the HIV/AIDS epidemic first claimed the world's attention as a health problem. Discrimination against carriers of HIV emerged with the first diagnoses and was immediately much more widespread than the virus itself. But the primary work of AIDS activists worldwide has focused less on rights than on the struggle to save lives by controlling the incidence and spread of the disease. As in the case of abortion advocacy, common ground and political alliances may be more productive if constructed on the basis of a health rationale rather than asserting the rights of persons with HIV/AIDS.

Like the myths about women's sexuality that surround abortion, the AIDS crisis has engendered fallacies that point to women, particularly prostitutes and sexually active women, as carriers of the virus. In fact, many of the world's women are powerless to protect themselves from HIV and the other sexually transmitted diseases that compound the risk of HIV transmission. Gender subordination keeps women locked into relationships in which their partners won't use condoms (at the micro-level), and it excludes women from decision-making bodies that set policies to address the crisis (at the macro-level). Nevertheless, women have been on the front lines in dealing with the epidemic as primary caretakers, and increasingly in many parts of the world, women are becoming a primary risk group.

In response to the AIDS epidemic, women have mobilized around sexual politics. Feminist efforts are primarily responsible for the widespread publicizing of the effects of STDs on women's health and their role in HIV transmission, as the controversy about Africa's 'infertility belt' attests (McFadden 1992). At the same time, AIDS has prompted the public self-affirmation of many homosexual groups in regions where they had previously been clandestine, such as Africa and Asia; these groups also promote greater awareness of sexual politics and human rights.

What does the spread of HIV via the sex industry have to do with human rights? In the South, the flourishing sex industry is a direct result of post-colonial agrarian and industrial policies that forced subsistance and small farmers off the land to become migrant labourers in plantation, extractive or capital-intensive industries. After destroying their self-sufficiency in food production in favour of export-oriented agro-industry, governments turned to tourism as a source of badly needed foreign exchange.

Women, left behind by husbands who migrated, have found that local agriculture became unviable as soils were depleted by mono-culture. They too have been forced to migrate, usually to urban centres. There, as the unskilled women enter the cash economy, they are forced to accept the lowest-paid jobs. For many, the only alternative to unemployment has been prostitution – servicing either the male workers displaced from their families or the growing tourist industries in major cities. At the same time, male migrants seek sex workers when away from home, returning to their wives to spread the virus.[22]

The displacement of workers and the growing sex industry are human rights issues that underlie the spread of HIV, but they are not the only factors responsible for the spread of the AIDS epidemic in the South. Dr Catherine Akidi Lore (1993), of Kenya, has identified a series of practices that may violate women's bodily integrity and may also contribute to the spread of the virus in Africa: abrasions during normal coital friction with a 'dry vagina', preferred by many men; perineal ulcers or wounds associated with early post-partum sex; shared circumcision instruments for girls;[23] wife/widow inheritance and polygamous marriages.[24] None of the above factors can be addressed either as a rights or health issue alone.

In sum, abortion and AIDS are just two cases in which both rights and health dimensions must be addressed simultaneously in order to avert further harm to women.

Challenges to the implementation of the reproductive health and rights framework

In addition to developing political strategies for policies that integrate the health and rights dimensions of women's reproduction, the women's movement now must also hold states accountable for adopting programmes to implement the policies as outlined by the ICPD document. In particular, women should differentiate between governments' appropriation of reproductive rights language and substantial policies that demonstrate comprehension and incorporation of women's health and rights concerns. Even where governments genuinely accept the need for change, applying the reproductive rights framework in practice will be a major challenge and should be closely monitored by the women's movement. Entrenched cultural practices, inequitable gender systems enshrined in the law and financial investment in the status quo may all stand in the way. At the three levels of culture, the state, and the marketplace, serious challenges remain to implementing the framework in all of the world's regions. Just some of the complexities of those challenges are discussed in the following sections.

Cultural biases and practices

The framework's emphasis on individual autonomy is Western. Acknowledging the concept of a relational 'self' would strengthen its relevance in diverse cultural contexts.

Many Southern activists and researchers assert that a Western development paradigm spawned the feminist concern for individual 'ownership' of the female body and autonomous control over reproductive functions. The related concept of bodily integrity is contested as founded in Western capitalist assumptions of self-ownership that imply a patriarchal, bourgeois concept of a discrete 'self' that may be subjugated by medical science, population control or patriarchal kinship systems.[25] The individualism and possession of the body, as well the power dimension implied in a concept of autonomous control (and, therefore, individual choice) are criticized as culturally biased notions inappropriate for many Southern women, particularly in Asia and Africa.

Participants in the Women's Global Network for Reproductive Rights 1993 India meeting concluded that the 'self' cannot be isolated from larger social conditions – conditions that often, in fact, determine which choices become available to women:

> Putting free choice central to reproductive rights leaves too much room to interpret it at an individual level and thus completely bypasses the level of society as a whole. As such, 'choice' reflects the dominant view of individualism in the West, more than anything else. Choice on its own, without attention to the context, has no value. For reproductive rights campaigns, emphasis should be on the conditions which determine the scope for reproductive self determination ... increased choice is offered without questioning the type of goods on the market, the market and market relations, and without raising the issue that more goods and services are not equal to more access or improved reproductive health conditions.[26]

As we have discussed, DAWN affirms that the 'self' reaches far beyond the notion of bodily integrity and must be understood in the context of all significant family, cultural, social and economic relationships. But the decision-making self must remain at the core of reproductive rights (with bodily integrity), and our challenge now is to expand the framework without demolishing this conceptual cornerstone. Toward this end, Obermeyer (1993) enquires,

> could it be that despite the inegalitarian principles on which they are based, traditional kinship groups offer a certain degree of security to females, and if so, then is it possible to improve reproductive choice without indiscriminately rejecting structures that provide important bases of identity and constitute a buffer between individuals and societal forces?

With Obermeyer, many activists and scholars in both the North and the South are exploring means of expanding the framework by conceptualizing how the actions of collective identities may be understood through holistic analyses of reproduction and reproductive labour. Among them, the IRRRAG network is drawing upon thousands of women's experiences in seven countries to develop such an expanded formulation of reproductive rights.

A second critique of the Western foundation of the reproductive rights framework draws upon an extreme cultural relativist position that 'emphasizes the different cultural and moral patterns prevailing in distinct cultures, and challenges the concept of human rights as a new form of imperialism' (Dalcero 1992). In so far as governments (such as China, most recently) claim that their sovereignty is threatened by the imposition of international human rights standards, they may formally assume such a posture regarding women's rights. Moreover, the perceived imposition of culturally 'insensitive' human rights standards may spark reactions to protect national sovereignty that even further endanger women's safety and health.

Fundamentalist activism may be only the most blatant example of how nationalist tensions may cause harm to women. National or 'traditional' identities take many forms, but they represent political uses of religion, not religious doctrine itself. Islam, for example, does not dictate women's oppression; fundamentalist political movements do. To demonstrate this case, Hélie-Lucas identifies the diversity of women's legal rights among Muslim countries:

> Tunisia offers both contraception and free abortion services to women; and in Bangladesh there is forced contraception, abortion and steriliza-

tion. Algeria, on the other hand, refused for 20 years even to allow knowledge about contraception and abortion. In 1984, Algerian women lost the right to marry. They now have to be given in marriage by a Wali (matrimonial tutor) and are considered minors throughout their lives. In all these countries, political leaders pretend to act in conformity with Islam while they are simply imposing a political solution on their population problems ... Islamic states turn to their only specificity – making women the guardians of culture and religion and confining them to a model and a way of life which is 14 centuries old.[27]

State failure to prosecute abuse of women is another way in which nationalism or preservation of national identity may underpin violations of women's rights. In India and China, for example, in an astounding example of how traditional culture and the state collude to ratify gender violence, governments ignore the selective abortion of female foetuses. The International Women's Rights Action Watch (IWRAW) cites a study in which

51 percent of families (in the Salem district of Tamil Nadu, India) had committed female infanticide in the last two years. Health and education programmes of the Indian government provided information and access to ultrasound and amniocentesis. Other village surveys found that the proportion of women in the general population is declining [see also Sen 1990] ... Female infanticide and post-ultrasound and post-amniocentesis abortions are becoming more prevalent in Asia, in countries such as South Korea, China, India and Bangladesh.[28]

The Southern women's perspective remains sensitive to cultural diversity and national sovereignty, and respects the consolidation of traditions that enhance and preserve cultural identity. Yet, again, perpetuating traditional or new forms of abuse of women's bodies and autonomy cannot fulfil that purpose. DAWN researchers from Asia, Africa and Latin America have identified state-sanctioned 'cultural' norms and practices hostile to women's freedom and equality in all of the world's regions. And in each region the question has been repeated: How can feminist values be combined with cultural identity?

In reply, DAWN's African researchers have reminded us that traditions are not static but historical processes; as 'traditional' beliefs and practices evolve, new patterns replace the old. Women's changing roles must be viewed in this context to transform and consolidate new forms of cultural identity that value women's intellectual, spiritual and material contributions to their societies.

Official delegates at the Cairo and Beijing UN conferences will be called upon to debate whether reproductive rights are inalienable natural rights or socially determined rights (i.e., reflecting the equality or inequality of gender relations that prevail in most societies). Embedded in those debates, the universality of woman's individual autonomy will be questioned and compared to the value of national sovereignty. At the 1993 UN Human Rights Conference in Vienna, the question arose once again: do 'universal' human rights standards and values exist? Delegates adopted a moderate final position, recognizing cultural variation in the definition of rights (and, therefore, rights abuses). That is, they found that human rights may be socially determined. This sort of outcome in Cairo and Beijing could be disastrous for the consolidation of women's rights worldwide. Women must organize coordinated strategies to ensure that women's universal human rights are affirmed in 1994 and 1995.

Facile polarization of 'traditional' and 'modern' systems may not account for resources women draw from cultural norms and practices.

Advocates of the reproductive health and rights framework frequently point to traditionalism as a barrier to the recognition of women's rights as full citizens in many Southern societies. DAWN researchers have observed that the traditional/modern dichotomy often employed to denounce gender violence fails to recognize 'traditional' women's strategies to protect and enhance their individual and collective strengths *within their cultures*. At the Africa regional DAWN meeting, one researcher suggested that local forms of female resistance to detrimental practices and patriarchal assumptions should be identified and valued, rather than applying foreign models of change, particularly in regard to sexual behaviour. Adetoun Ilumoka (1993) expands on this point by seeking momentum for change within local practices:

The challenge before women in Africa, especially those who are relatively empowered to bring about change, is how to tap existing forms of resistance and learn from positive aspects of old modes of social organizations which are identifiable. We need to be careful how we use the loaded language of rights, whilst also developing innovative approaches and perhaps a different, less alienating language apppropriate to the search for enduring solutions to our problems.

Certain 'traditional' practices may be acceptable to women because they help them to meet their practical daily needs, even though they reinforce their subordination. For example, a few DAWN participants cited how co-wives in African societies may share reproductive responsibilities and moral support in childrearing, relieving women of the burden of exercising their individual 'autonomy' over the management of household resources. Seny Diagne elucidates this point:

> There is no doubt whatsoever that [polygamy] contributes to the violation of women's rights; but it is more or less accepted by African women. It is accepted by rural women because the arrival of a second wife means a certain lightening of their domestic burdens. City women are also coming to a greater acceptance of polygamy because for them it means liberation from the servitude of marriage; a wife can go about her own business when she is not on duty, without having to worry about the care and feeding of her husband. Should polygamy then be eliminated? I think that there should be an awareness-raising campaign to bring about change in customs and attitudes, while maintaining the progressive gains that have been made in certain countries, for instance in Senegal, where people have a right to choose between monogamy and polygamy.[29]

Many African women may accept polygamy as a practical solution to their already overburdened lives, but DAWN members agree that the practice does represent a negation of women's full personhood. In most of Latin America and the Caribbean, informal polygamous practices have been the rule for centuries. However, those regions' legal systems have outlawed polygamy, and women have also taken strategic actions to protect their conjugal rights – for example, to an equal share of household wealth and paternal responsibility for child maintenance. Until African women join women around the world to denounce polygamy along with other forms of conjugal subordination, gender relations cannot be structurally and strategically transformed.

DAWN affirms the crucial importance of cultural integrity and supports women's roles in the family's and community's daily rituals that both reinforce and renew cultural identity. However, when cultural practices only consolidate women's subordination, and damage women's physical integrity or their freedom to make decisions about their own lives, we must question them. Two extremely detrimental practices, among the many others found in all world cultures, are child marriage and genital mutilation. Both are widely practised across many cultures, and both are rooted in the idea that women, as the property of their male relatives, are more valuable to other males as sexual objects if they are sexually inexperienced virgins. For example, research on child marriage reveals that

> In Nigeria, one-quarter of all women are married by the age of fourteen, one-half by the age of sixteen and three-quarters by the age of 18. In that country and, for instance, Jamaica, women younger than fifteen years of age are four times more likely to die during pregancy and childbirth than women aged from fifteen to nineteen. In certain situations, adolescents may seek unskilled abortion, such as to avoid expulsion from school on grounds of pregnancy (Cook 1992).

Among other psychological and physical dangers, a major health risk associated with child marriage is obstructed labour because the baby's head is too big for the young mother's pelvis. The consequences of obstructed labour, particularly when the birth does not occur in a hospital (as in about 70 per cent of births in Nigeria, for example) are vesico-vaginal fistula (VVF), recto-vaginal fistula (RV) and reproductive tract infections. The fistulae are caused by the prolonged pressure of the baby's head in the vaginal canal and later result in leakage of urine or faeces, or both, through the vagina. Young women victims of VVF and RV become outcasts because of their incontinence. Often these women are divorced by their husbands because they cannot bear children (Cook 1993).

SEXUAL AND REPRODUCTIVE HEALTH AND RIGHTS / 83

Health risks are not the only reason why children should not be expected to marry. In contexts where child marriage is prevalent, girls are usually 'given' in marriage to a husband chosen by their families. Young women have the right to seek education and economic autonomy, if they wish, before being saddled with reproductive responsibilities. In any case, a woman's decision to marry, and to whom, should be her own.

In the case of female genital mutilation, we acknowledge that interpretations of the significance of this practice are diverse.[30] At the African DAWN Regional Meeting, some participants viewed female 'circumcision' as a clear violation of bodily integrity and an attempt to control female sexuality, while others understood the practice as a means of valuing and protecting girls' virginity, and, therefore, their sexuality. A third view interpreted it as a social mechanism to protect girls from males unable to control their sexuality. Finally, in some cultures, female 'circumcision' is a rite of passage for adolescents – a way women gain power in their community by demonstrating they can withstand high levels of pain.

As attention to female genital mutilation increases among Western governments and the Western press,[31] many African women are concerned that efforts to work within their cultural and political systems to eradicate the practice are undermined by sensationalism and portraying Africans as primitive. In an op-ed piece in the *New York Times* (7 December 1993), two African professional women, Seble Dawit and Salem Mekuria, stated that 'genital mutilation does not exist in a vacuum but as part of the social fabric, stemming from the power imbalance in relations between the sexes'. They concluded that the most effective way to eradicate the practice is to 'forge partnerships with the hundreds of African women on the continent who are working' along these lines, helping to 'create room for them to speak, and to speak with us as well'.[32]

DAWN seeks to open channels for dialogue on the range of issues sensitive to women's identity. In addition to child marriage and female 'circumcision', other practices rooted in the idea of women as property, such as bride price in Asia, the Pacific and

Africa, and dowry in India, are deeply controversial and often go to the heart of women's identification with their communities. Despite our diverse understandings of these practices, DAWN's consensus is that the facile dichotomization of traditional/modern categories may impede dialogue and mutual comprehension among women. DAWN affirms that much of what is viewed as 'traditional' should be preserved. However, the full force of the law should be applied to protect women suffering from unwanted violence to their personal integrity.

The challenges discussed above reflect how culture and religion may interact with political systems to prevent women from exercising their full citizenship. In the following section, we discuss how states' legal systems and institutions may further consolidate women's subordination.

Challenges posed by state systems
Heterogeneous systems of statutory and customary law operate simultaneously in many settings, often contradicting reproductive rights principles.

A serious barrier to implementing the reproductive health and rights framework in many countries will be the persistence of practices that are harmful to women but justified by customary legal systems. Participants in the DAWN meetings identified the widespread conflicts between statutory legal systems and customary codes as one of their most demanding challenges.

In some countries, even when laws protecting women's rights are on the statute books, violations in the name of religion or tradition are frequent and go unpunished, especially in Asia and Africa. This problem is rooted in the lack of a tradition of civil law, in many settings, and the corruption and/or inefficiency of state institutions such as the police and judiciary. In cases of former colonies, neo-colonial legal systems may explicitly contradict customary laws and therefore do not represent the interests of the population, and much less those of women. The spread of political conservatism and fundamentalism in the last two decades – with their own elaborate alternative legal systems – has further deepened enforcement problems.

The gap between abortion laws and practices worldwide is probably the most striking example of the contradiction. In Brazil, for example, 1942 legislation permitted abortion in cases of rape or risk to the mother's life. However, the public health system provided services for women legally entitled to an abortion only in 1989, in response to an order from the São Paulo Municipal Health Department (Araújo 1993). In many countries abortion is illegal under any circumstances, but, as in Kenya, is widely practised with the full knowledge of public authorities. In some cases, such as Bangladesh, abortion is accepted by customary legal systems, but is a crime under statutory law. Finally, in the last decade we have seen that even where abortion has been fully legal, as in the USA, Germany, Poland, Croatia and Russia, neo-conservative social forces may roll back women's hard-won access to safe abortion.

Given these contradictory legal situations in virtually all world regions and in regard to a number of other rights issues – including rights as elementary as voting and freedom of movement – DAWN calls for an explicit provision in the reproductive rights framework stating that statutory *and* customary legal systems will be held to account for violations of women's fundamental human rights.

The cornerstone of the framework, individual autonomy, is dependent upon a series of enabling conditions.

We have discussed how the notion of choice may be meaningless in contexts where enabling conditions are absent. Women are unable fully to exercise their human rights whenever their livelihood is endangered, public health and education systems are inadequate and cultural diversity is not respected. These social and economic rights dimensions represent the enabling conditions necessary for women to feel they can influence the direction of events in their lives, and they are particularly crucial when class, race and ethnic inequalities are also present (Corrêa and Petchesky 1994).

DAWN researchers have suggested that the language of the reproductive rights framework must firmly place social and economic rights within the larger context of human rights and social justice. A Southern feminist construction of effective reproductive choice requires that this so-called second generation of human rights be officially recognized, to include adequate nutrition, housing, a job and social assistance (i.e., education, day-care, health care and contraception) in the roster of basic human rights. This vital element is missing from the official agencies' approach to reproductive health and rights, as well as from the official women's rights instruments.

The population establishment's first sensitivity toward women's more comprehensive needs was incorporated in the *quality of care* movement of the 1980s. The term has a hybrid origin. It simultaneously drew upon the *total quality* movement in private enterprise and the feminist critiques of population policies.

Judith Bruce first delineated the framework in *Fundamental Elements of the Quality of Care* (Bruce 1990). The approach includes: choice among a range of contraceptive methods; availability of full information about all methods and their side-effects; providers' technical competence combined with interpersonal skills; structural incentives for maintaining availability of an appropriate constellation of services.

The hypothesis underlying the quality-of-care approach was that better quality would result in user-friendly services, thereby assuring greater contraceptive acceptance, continuity and higher 'success' rates.[33] It is almost entirely focused on individual fertility management through delivery systems that are isolated from a comprehensive health programme. The framework also fails to address the impact of broader social processes on the health system, such as drastically reduced funding for public services, migration of professionals to urban areas, discrimination and other forms of social disadvantage that limit poor women's access to services.[34]

From a Southern feminist perspective, an appropriate constellation of reproductive health services should encompass, in addition to the elements included in the quality-of-care framework, a quality approach to pre- and postnatal care, full gynaecological services, cervical and breast cancer screening, STD/RTI prevention (with special attention to HIV/AIDS) and safe abortion services (or at the minimum, adequate treatment for women who have suffered an incomplete abortion). A truly comprehensive approach would also include assistance to adolescents and women during menopause and, in many settings, mental health and occupational health services. DAWN researchers have also suggested that this basic constellation of services should be even further broadened to address sexuality and rape and other forms of gender violence.

Support for enabling conditions reflects the Southern feminist view that the dichotomy between women's biological and social reproductive functions is artificial. Therefore, a number of social rights should be added to the above constellation of appropriate services: guaranteed minimum nutritional intake, childcare centres, basic education, conditions that make maternity leave and breast-feeding viable for working mothers, and public services to facilitate household maintenance.

We are well aware of the challenges of implementing such a comprehensive constellation of services in diverse cultural and political settings. However, our blueprint for change is no more audacious than the Malthusian utopia must have appeared when social engineers drew up their plans to orchestrate the fertility decline of the entire world's women. And embedded in our proposal is a radical critique of the renewed political emphasis on market solutions to social problems.

Challenges of the marketplace

In Southern countries, we recognize an alarming trend away from state responsibility for basic needs. Market forces have increasingly been employed to mobilize and distribute health resources that should be widely available to the public. Based on structural adjustment policies, this tendency towards privatizing the health sector isolates it from other basic services (which, in many cases, are also being privatized) and limits even further poor women's access to health care. A 1993 national study of municipal health services in Brazil found, for example, that in at least one-quarter of all Brazilian cities, less than 10 per cent of the target population had access to basic women's health services (Costa 1992).

Limited data are available to document the impact on women's health indicators of states' shrinking investments in health. To respond more effectively to the spreading neo-liberal approach to health marketing, women's research must demonstrate convincingly how the approach has cost women's lives around the world.

Compounding the questions of resource distribution, the private sector's aggressive testing and marketing of new medical technologies has aggravated women's social subordination by appropriating control over their bodies and their health knowledge.

NEW REPRODUCTIVE TECHNOLOGIES: SEPARATING THE WHEAT FROM THE CHAFF Ever since the eighteenth century, medical science has appropriated traditional knowledge of women healers – whether midwifery, 'witchcraft' or herbal and spiritual techniques. In contrast to traditional practices that seek balance among the physical, spiritual and natural realms, medicine aggressively seeks control over the human body and its functions. Women's bodies have historically served as objects of medical control, particularly in the development and testing of contraceptive and reproductive technologies.

The chaff DAWN focuses its critique of reproductive technology in three major areas:

1. Contraceptive development and delivery, particularly the ethical questions surrounding the testing of medically risky products exclusively in the South and among marginalized risk groups:

Contraceptive development has historically depended upon clinical trials conducted among poor and Southern women. The newest contraceptive technology (now being tested in Southern countries) is the contraceptive vaccine. This method is a systemic (rather than hormonal) intervention intended to prevent pregnancy for up to six months. It targets the immunological system in order to block the production of gonadotrophins, which sustain the development of the embryo. Aside from the considerable potential risks of intervening in the body's immunological response, DAWN also questions the ethical responsibility of investing millions of dollars in developing such a method, given the urgency of researching the human immunological response to HIV.

An example of the problems associated with *contraceptive delivery* is the case of the long-acting hormonal implant, Norplant, which has been distributed all over the world. Norplant was given to village women in Indonesia by poorly trained medical personnel who often failed to maintain aseptic conditions when the device was inserted (Ward et al. 1992). Some of the village women understood they would be punished if they didn't accept the implant, and most were unaware of potential side effects or that the device was removable (Boland et al. 1994).

A third case illustrates the importance of distinguishing between medical risks of a new technology versus the risks associated with inappropriate delivery and follow-up: the delivery of IUDs in Brazil. In the early 1970s, IUDs (including the Dalkon Shield, the Copper-7 and Lippe's Loop) were introduced. But providers supplied no information about possible side effects and no follow-up was scheduled. Some doctors even refused to withdraw the device. Thus, the disastrous problems many women experienced led Brazilian women to reject all IUDs, which are now among the least prevalent contraceptive methods in Brazil. Women's experiences with many other contraceptive methods may be similarly analysed, and current testing of the AIDS vaccine in Southern countries must be challenged in the same light.

2. Excessive medical interventions such as caesarean sections, unnecessary surgery, etc: In its attempt to gain control over the human body, the medical establishment frequently ignores the human capacity for self-healing. Instead, physicians recommend provider-controlled technologies which inevitably are more profitable than non-interventionist treatment. The prime example of this trend is the soaring rates of caesarean births in the North and the South.

Another dramatic example is the increasing use of amniocentesis to detect foetal gender. Originally designed as a resource for early detection of birth defects or to diagnose risks to mothers' health, amniocentesis is widely used in Asia to terminate pregnancies when a female child is unwanted. While in countries such as India and Bangladesh cultural circumstances may lead women to seek the technology, in other settings such as China, the government's strict one-child policy compounds the cultural preference for male children.[35]

3. New reproductive technologies (NRTs), such as assisted fertility and genetic testing: From a Southern perspective, excessive medical intervention on the one hand and the total lack of basic health care on the other represents a profound contradiction in how health resources are distributed. The problem applies to North–South inequalities as well as to class differences within all countries. In fact, women's health status is determined less by the availability of medical technology than by their social and economic conditions, gender, race and class status. In Brazil, for example, the world's most modern contraceptives and fertility services are available, and more women have caesarean sections than in any other country. Yet, each year over a million women deliver children without having had a single pre-natal check-up.

The rapid expansion of NRTs in the South follows this pattern, as sophisticated procedures become ever more available to the wealthy, alongside the absolute absence of basic health services for the majority of women. Angela Davis (1991) analyses this worldwide trend:

> Although the new reproductive technologies cannot be construed as inherently affirmative or violative of women's reproductive rights, the anchoring of the technologies to the profit schemes of their producers and distributors results in a commodification of motherhood that complicates and deepens power relationships based on class and gender ... Moreover, the ideology of motherhood is wedded to an obdurate denial of the very social services women require in order to make meaningful choices to bear or not bear children.

Southern feminists are concerned about a second set of problems associated with NRTs: genetic testing and assisted fertility techniques may potentially be employed for genetic engineering purposes. This area has not been explored in depth, but it may represent a real future danger. We have already discussed how population control policies have been applied to limit unwanted ethnic groups in the Pacific, China, South Africa, North America, Brazil and elsewhere, and we have discussed how amniocentesis has been applied to select foetal gender in several Asian settings.

With the contemporary rise of militant racist and neo-fascist groups in many parts of the North, we have no reason to believe that such groups would not attempt to 'screen out' unwanted genetic or ethnic 'types' – such as the darker-skinned, people of Semitic descent, the disabled or homosexuals – from the population. Such potential perverse uses of NRTs must be considered and averted now, at the design stage of technology development.

The wheat As detrimental as modern medicine has been to women, DAWN recognizes that medical technology offers women a great deal and must not be rejected wholesale. Until the twentieth century, maternity killed millions of young women. As discussed earlier in this chapter, maternal mortality is still a major killer in Southern countries.

The improvement of maternal–child health programmes in order to avoid more deaths is a central feminist demand. Any women who has suffered a backstreet abortion will agree that today's safer and less painful abortion techniques are welcome. The same may be said for cancer and STD screening and treatments. A Brazilian feminist, Margareth Arilha (1993) believes that assisted fertility must also be admitted to the roster of reproductive rights:

> The possibility for women and men to have 'genetic children' and apparently solve their infertility is born out of the ... social rejection concerning maternity/paternity failures ... But it is impossible to deny that this technological solution can be assimilated as something that may bring fulfilment and be constructed as a right.

Examples abound of unethical scientific developments and practices, but it is equally clear that scientists from diverse disciplines have raised ethical concerns about their own work and have initiated mechanisms to establish ethical principles to guide scientific research. The Helsinki Agreement on biomedical research is just one example.

Despite such accords, scientists, policy makers and feminists continue to be locked in conflict over reproductive technologies, making communication ever more difficult. Dialogue is possible, however, as recent debates about contraceptive development demonstrate. Since 1986, feminists and scientists have held meetings within and between various countries (including the USA, Brazil, Peru, India and the Philippines). To be sure, results have been uneven, and an objective and comprehensive assessment of these attempts has yet to be made. Nevertheless, such efforts cannot be considered to have been in vain.

To summarize the major arguments of this chapter, the reproductive rights and health framework has evolved conceptually over at least fifteen years. In the process, the international women's movement drew upon human rights principles to remove women's reproduction from its isolation, placing it in the larger context of equitable development policies to provide for basic social and material needs, including freedom from abuse, comprehensive health services, education and employment. Now that the framework has been debated and adopted by powerful institutions, DAWN recognizes the risk that feminist discourse may be appropriated and manipulated by the population control, development and scientific communities; we call for Southern women critically to distinguish institutional discourse from substantive policies and interventions that in fact further women's rights to health and well-being.

Our next major challenge will be to forge a new development paradigm incorporating women's rights. Therefore, we call for new dialogue and stronger alliances with the development community, in the spirit of the remarkably effective ICPD process.

Even as we celebrate the victory of an ICPD draft document that reflects our interests, the challenges of implementing the framework lie ahead. First, DAWN strongly endorses the importance of cultural identity and traditions that enhance women's well-being. Yet we urge Southern women to recognize that claims of cultural relativism or moral supremacy, often in the name of preserving cultural or national sovereignty or religion, may weaken women's position regarding the defence of their universally recognized rights.

Second, we call for women to hold their states accountable for providing adequate services and protecting women's basic rights, and for reforming their legal frameworks in order to do so. Towards that end, they must bring customary and statutory law into alignment and improve enforcement mechanisms.

Third, we question the neo-liberal ideology that promotes the marketplace as the provider for basic human needs.

In sum, we stand for the freedom of all women to make life choices – unchecked by cultural restrictions, legal or economic barriers – allowing them to realize their full humanity in all of the diverse ways that women may envision it.

Notes

1. Also in Pakistan, a woman must produce four male witnesses in order to press charges against a rapist. If she cannot come up with the satisfactory eyewitness evidence, she risks being charged herself with *Zina* (fornication, if unmarried, and adultery if married) and sentenced to three years imprisonment. See Coomaraswamy 1992.

2. CEDAW's main advance over previous instruments was that it called upon states to recognize the equality of men and women, women's rights to vote, to choose a profession, and to entitlements such as schooling and employment. Perhaps most significant, CEDAW included an affirmative action clause: 'temporary special measures aimed at accelerating *de facto* equality between men and women' ... to be discontinued 'when the objective of equality of opportunity and treatment have been achieved' (Appendix A, Article 4, Part I).

3. As of January 1993, 119 governments had become signatories to CEDAW.

4. Freedman and Isaacs (1993) note that this statement was probably intended to convince governments to implement family planning rather than to protect the rights of women from population control.

5. In fact, the family planning movement promoted the principles ratified in Tehran and Bucharest in order to support its efforts to disseminate

contraception globally, bypassing national resistances. It is interesting to note that at that time and for many years to follow, the movement strove to maintain an image of a liberal social force, opposed to conservative actors embodied by the Catholic Church, traditional religious leaders and culturally conservative political forces.

6. 'A UN Symposium on Population and Human Rights held in Vienna in 1981 declared that, "Both the compulsory use of abortion and its unqualified prohibition would be a serious violation of human rights," and the three international conferences associated with the UN Decade for Women (Mexico City, 1975; Copenhagen, 1980; Nairobi, 1985) were more evasive in their recommendations, however, perhaps in large part because delegates were officially appointed representatives of their governments ... in the official conferences the principle of reproductive rights beyond the familiar "right to family planning" does not appear in the plans of action adopted at each conference' (Dixon-Mueller 1990: 308).

7. The previous year in the United States, the term 'reproductive rights' had first come into use – but was not fully defined – when the Committee for Abortion Rights and Against Sterilization Abuse was founded in 1977 to oppose a congressional amendment that curtailed government funds for abortions for poor women (see Petchesky and Weiner 1990).

8. The meeting began to define the political agenda of subsequent years, which would include debates about diverse cultural and political interpretations of the rights concepts, revisions of its recommendations, and a forum for divergent views within the international women's health movement. It also inaugurated a series of International Feminist Reproductive Rights events – in Costa Rica (1987), Manila (1990), and Kampala (1993) – and sparked the creation of regional and country-based networks. The networks have effectively disseminated information and strategies to mobilize women around the world.

9. In some contexts, reproductive rights activists and the population establishment were even able to hald dialogues and collaborate for specific political ends, although such partnerships often created controversies.

10. DAWN's membership holds differing opinions on how to address this issue. Some wholly reject the reproductive health framework because it focuses only on women's maternal roles, arguing in favor of a comprehensive health services approach instead. In response, other DAWN researchers cite that family planning services are the only health services available in their countries, especially for rural women, and are thus badly needed. In still other cases, such as Egypt, comprehensive health services have eroded as the family planning industry took over the existing health infrastructure. Most DAWN researchers agreed with the approach of the Brazilian women's

movement which promotes a *women's* health framework rather than diverging over comprehensive versus reproductive health approaches. In any case, the specific strategy must be adapted according to different country contexts. But it is important that in all contexts women's health rights be introduced into the public sphere as a state obligation, rather than hidden in the private realm where women are forced to rely on inadequate resources or unscrupulous providers.

11. See also Griffen 1994.

12. Cited in Smyth 1991.

13. At the same time, the framework totally ignores men's reproductive responsibilities.

14. While reproductive health and rights activists have concentrated a great deal of attention on the population establishment's co-opting of feminist language, they have failed to call attention to similar strategies used by anti-abortion forces. Unfettered by 'copyright complaints' from feminists, the right-to-life movement has freely appropriated the discourse of feminist critiques of population and development policies.

15. Data on historical and more recent demographic transition processes indicate that abortion continues to play a key role in fertility reduction around the world.

16. Dixon-Mueller 1993: 307; see also *International Journal of Gynecology and Obstetrics*, Supplement 3: 175, 1989.

17. With its infamous 'Mexico City Policy' in 1984, a US administration under pressure from the right-to-life movement prohibited any foreign assistance to organizations offering abortion services. Although scientific research on abortion was not banned, studies of the health consequences of abortion and operations research were set back for nearly a decade (Sundstrom, 1993: 49).

18. In Africa and Latin America, only Tunisia and Cuba permit abortion on request. In Kenya and Nigeria it is illegal but widely practised in clinics and even advertised in the public media.

19. However, right-to-life groups in those countries have organized increasingly successful anti-abortion campaigns.

20. As McKinnon (1993) states: 'because forced maternity is sex equality deprivation, legal abortion is sex equality rights.'

21. The International Reproductive Rights Research Action Group (IRRRAG) is investigating these questions in each of the world's regions.

22. Consequences of this process in Africa are described in greater detail by McHale: 'The changes wrought by development (the introduction of logging, roads, railways and the establishment of plantations) have disrupted ecological areas, impoverished the rural areas, led to an introduction of other

health problems and a decline in nutritional levels leading to acute and chronic malnutrition and depressed immune systems. The reliance on cash crops for export and the displacement of Africans from the best land are major contributors to malnutrition, which increases susceptibility to infection. This problem is common to many of the African countries with the highest number of cases of AIDS (Kenya, Zambia, Zaire, Tanzania)', in McHale and Choong 1989. See also Orubuloye, Caldwell and Caldwell, 1993.

23. However, Mann et al. (1988) found that 'the countries in which female circumcision is most common are not in general those where HIV or AIDS is most prevalent'.

24. Participants in the DAWN Caribbean Regional Meeting identified several factors that contribute to the spread of the human immuno-deficiency virus in common with those cited by Dr Lore.

25. Petchesky undertook a historical review of how the European notion of the body as 'property' developed out of the notion of common access, communitarian notions of rights of *access to* property and individual freedoms into the dominant patriarchal notion of *ownership as 'having'* property. She cites Patricia Hill Collins' concept of African American women's alternative notion of the extended self that is nevertheless 'self'-defined: 'the ethic of black women's bodily integrity as communal and extended rather than individualized and privatized.' Petchesky concludes that 'we can recognize the historical coherence of self-ownership as a moral and political claim without subscribing to any essentialist assumptions about fixed or transcendent subjects', viewing our 'selves' not just as bodies but attached to a physical trajectory.

26. Women's Global Network for Reproductive Rights 1993c. See also Nair 1993.

27. Helie-Lucas 1993. Carla Makhlouf Obermeyer concurs: 'The variability in levels of socio-economic development in Muslim countries means that there are great discrepancies in the social reality of women's autonomy, both between countries and within the same country between different parts of the population. Consequently, it is impossible to assign to Islam some kind of "score" that would provide a useful summary of women's autonomy ... There is no centralized authoritative interpretation of religious doctrine; instead there are decentralized and sometimes dissimilar traditions embodied in the various schools of law and religious sects ... The same texts can be used to legitimate very divergent views: a literal interpretation could provide the basis for justifying women's subordinate position, while reformers have at different periods argued that (the inegalitarian elements in Islam) should be reinterpreted in light of contemporary conditions' (Obermeyer 1994). See also Coomaraswamy 1992.

28. IWRAW, *The Women's Watch*, Vol. 7, No. 3, January 1994.

29. Diagne 1993. Adams and Castle (1994) further illustrate how complex the dynamics of West African polygamous households can be, describing how social, economic, and power relationships among women *within* households may influence reproductive behavior in contradictory ways: 'Differences among women relate mainly to inequalities in access to or control over nonmaterial resources, such as time, information, and labor within the domestic domain ... Polygyny may ... benefit the reproductive health of women and the health and nutrition of children by facilitating prolonged post-partum sexual abstinence ... In some cases, women play out ... rivalries (among co-wives) within the domain of reproduction, using children as political pawns to further their objectives within the household economy ... In Sierra Leone, conflicts among co-wives over the educational prospects of their respective children have led to accusations of witchcraft, or to senior women's assigning arduous chores to the children of more junior co-wives. In the same setting, co-wives were noted to decrease their duration of breastfeeding to hasten their return to fecundability, in hopes of 'outdoing' rival wives in terms of the number of offspring they produced for their husband.' The authors cite Bledsoe (1987) as the source of the data from Sierra Leone.

30. It is not known how prevalent it is; estimates range from 70 to 170 million. Campaigns to abolish the practice, sometimes led by village chiefs, have been successful in some areas.

31. In November 1993, the French government prosecuted a woman from Mali accused of allowing her three-month-old daughter to be subjected to genital mutilation. In the last decade in France a growing number of girls have been admitted to hospitals with health complications due to genital mutilation. The debate continues over whether the French government has the right to interfere with customary practices among immigrant communities.

32. Cited in IWRAW, *Women's Watch*, Vol. 7, No. 3, January 1994.

33. This is a classic example in which feminist concepts and discourse were assimilated (and diluted) by the population establishment.

34. Moreover, the success of the 'quality' component of the approach has been difficult to measure, as its ingredients are subjective.

35. At least two Chinese citizens have applied to the US for political asylum on grounds of fearing repercussions for violating China's one-child policy.

3 Forward-looking strategies: beyond Cairo

Since we published *Development, Crises, and Alternative Visions: Third World Women's Perspectives* in 1987, most of the limits to development we identified still apply, but some of the issues and strategies proposed in that book require new critical assessment. In 1987, we urged that women's voices should take part on the definition of development and the making of policy choices; in the economic sphere, we advocated long-term strategies to break down structures of inequality between genders, classes and nations, which act as barriers to development; we alerted women to the importance of reorienting production to meet the needs of the poor and of making women central to both planning and implementation of production; we advocated national self-reliance, reductions in military expenditures, and limits to multinational incursions into national economies; we requested that international bodies exert pressure in the areas of basic needs, land reform, technology, women's work and employment, and national and international systems of data collection and planning.

As strategies to reach those goals, we proposed an international feminist research agenda; regional training and research programmes to strengthen women's organizations and women's roles in policy development; national cross-sectoral coalitions to promote women's interests; support for public education on women's issues using popular culture, informal education and mass media, and significant reforms in formal education.

In 1994, some of those strategies have partially succeeded and the international scenario has changed profoundly. A bi-polar power struggle no longer dictates worldwide strategic interests and political alliances. In this context, *development* may be evolving toward a new meaning. While development aid is still manipulated for political and market-oriented purposes, new political actors representing civil society are now seizing an unprecedented moment to break into the world order. Activists all over the world are reshaping the purposes of world bodies and investing them with renewed authority to monitor and censure government complicity with gender, class and ethnic violence, structural inequality and other policies or practices that negatively affect women.

The UN Conference on Environment and Development (1992), the UN Conference on Human Rights (1993) and preparations for the ICPD have demonstrated that, as never before, the international women's community has finally established political legitimacy. But although women's concerns are now officially recognized, there is still a long way to go beyond Cairo to assure implementation and enforcement of our proposals. As we have illustrated, entrenched cultural traditions, obdurate states and fierce market mechanisms seem actually to collude to reinforce women's subordination around the world.

Therefore, in an attempt to ensure that the reproductive health and rights framework is implemented, the declaration of the Reproductive Health and Justice International Conference includes clear accountability mechanisms. Women's organizations and networks – national, regional and interregional – may refer to those mechanisms as we develop strategies for Cairo and beyond.

Strengthening the international women's movement

We must also take a critical look at problems that have impeded the productivity of the women's movement in the past and may continue to stand in the way of consolidating our recent gains. In 1987, we documented problems within the women's movement that limited effective strategy-formation. Among them we identified how, conceptually, the women's movement often confined its actions to the private domain or informal economy, rather than articulating clear links among mainstream development, economic issues and women's equality. We identified further faults in our search for non-hierarchical and non-formal organizational structures, discovering that women's difficulty in establishing power structures and asserting authority had weakened our ability to make an impact on public policies. Finally, we found that we needed to build alliances with other sectors of civil society and share power by widening our membership bases.

Many of the problems identified in 1987 have been addressed in the intervening years. Partially as a result of the past decade's revolution in information technology, the international women's movement has become a much more cohesive and articulate player on the world stage. In international fora such as the UN conferences, IMF and World Bank meetings and academic and international development conferences, feminists have disseminated coherent positions on women's human rights and the differential impacts of economic and development policies on women. These positions are supported by well-defined international women's constituencies.

This level of international representation has been possible because much of the women's movement has achieved organizational maturity, incorporating mechanisms for clear division of responsibilities and broader participation, and increasingly accessing global communications technologies. Around the world, women's organizations and networks have established alliances with the human rights and development communities, indigenous and gay and lesbian movements, and, in some cases, have engaged in ongoing dialogue with governmental sectors.

In spite of all those advances, a number of conceptual and ideological debates, as well as weaknesses in organizing strategies, continue to trouble the women's movement. Within DAWN, for example, we continue to debate whether we should propose that *comprehensive health services* be improved, or that specific *women's reproductive health services* are our primary goal. Proponents of the former position argue that better services for everyone will benefit women as well, while those arguing for women's services fear that women will get left out if they are not specifically targeted. Others point out that in many regions of the world, the *only* health services available to the poor are the family planning and maternal-child health facilities; if they are eliminated in favour of an ideal constellation of comprehensive services, the result may be no services at all.

A recent issue of *DAWN Informs* (Corrêa et al. 1994) ponders whether we are even asking the right questions, by focusing our debate so closely on reproduction. The authors also identify new and ongoing problems in women's organizing and political strategies. First, the women's movement has not paid sufficient attention to our diversity – of national identity, race, ethnicity and class. Our diversity is a reality, but perhaps because of the fear that acknowledging difference could divide our forces, our discourse and practice have not reflected that reality. A clear priority beyond Cairo is to articulate how our richly diverse make-up can become a means of strengthening our political legitimacy.

Just as some activists fear that acknowledging our diversity could divide us, some feminists are hanging on to the notion of radically opposed male–female identities. This separatist tendency polarizes feminist initiatives and limits our ability to explore potential alliances beyond the borders of the women's movement. Moreover, separatism raises the risk of isolating the movement, as it takes the principle of autonomy to its extreme.

A third area of continuing divergence is whether women should pursue a strategy of structural change versus the incremental transformation of institutions and social practices. Activists' attempts to influence population policies have sparked renewed controversy over this issue within the reproductive health and rights movement. Those who object to dialogue feel that the population and reproductive health approaches are too radically distinct to reach consensus on reform of population policies. Moreover, the imbalance of power between the population establishment and the women's movement does not bode well for feminist gains. Some activists have also voiced the need to deepen and consolidate a consensual feminist perspective before engaging in high-level power struggles with the population establishment. Finally, many women's rights activists maintain that the movement's principle of autonomy eliminates the option of negotiating alliances with the population establishment.

Box 3.1 Summary of the working group on political process –
Reproductive Health and Justice: International Women's Conference
for Cairo '94

1. *Linkages: who, what and how*

Who: We must build linkages within the women's movement;
between the movement and the government; between the movement
and the society at large; and among international networks.

What: Reproductive rights are not an isolated issue, but are intrinsically linked to macro-development models.

How: We need to ensure the link between strengthening the
movement internally (through information flow, transparency in
actions, feedback and monitoring) and external work (by creating
alternatives, advocating and lobbying policy-makers). To stress the
inter-connectedness of issues requires solidarity in support of each
other's actions.

2. *Mobilization for reproductive rights and justice* Reproductive
rights activists should not limit themselves to working with the
women's movement, but should link up with other social movements
locally, nationally and internationally.

3. *Working inside and outside the official ICPD process* Outsiders
have less power and need allies inside; insiders cannot do their work
properly if they have no backing from outsiders in the movement.
Distinguish among those outside because they are uninformed and
those outside for tactical reasons. Work inside if you are able to
maintain your own agenda, terms of reference and avoid co-optation.
Act with confidence and force: *both* are required.

4. *Dialogue and working with population institutions* 'Dialoguers'
and 'workers within' have to be explicit about their own women's
movement-backed agenda.

5. *Commitment and accountability within the movement* Privileged
political actors should take care to relate openly with women at the
grassroots level in the community, provide information and encourage
articulation of local needs and demands, and translate these into
more general political demands at the national and international
level.

6. *Representation* Actors at any level have to be responsible and
accountable to the women whose interests they represent. It is not
acceptable that powerful international bodies appoint (top-down)
so-called experts and women's representatives.

7. *Women and the state* NGOs have to hold governments accountable for promises they have made or conventions they have signed. This requires a public monitoring process.

8. *Donors* Distinguish between donors with their own agenda (making instrumental use of women) and donors willing to fund work as defined by women themselves.

9. *Transparency* Transparency means acknowledging and working with power differences, and it leads to cooperation in clearly defined, public and agreed-upon terms.

10. *Importance of vision and collectively developing a global conceptual and analytical framework for local, specific strategies and actions* To build the strength of the movement or of alliances, the time- and energy-consuming process of sharing experience and vision cannot be skipped.

11. *Assessment of our strength as a movement* On our various routes to Cairo, the movement-building and alliance-making process is going on. We know that advocacy will only be successful if there are solid local organizing efforts. We must have unity in our vision, and solidarity in our strategies. We will have political impact: our power-tools are diversity and subversion.

DAWN has participated actively in these debates and has decided to struggle to gather the forces necessary to exert power where power lies. We find that intervening to defend women's interests and rights does not mean we have abandoned a broader critique of the system's inequalities. But a decision not to intervene means leaving the control of power in the hands of others. These political strategies must be developed through constant dialogues within the movement and guided by clear ground rules: democratic decision-making processes, clear division of labour between those operating from within and those exerting pressures from outside dominant political systems, transparency and trust among ourselves.

With strong support from within the international women's movement, we are now advancing to transform gender systems at the levels of culture, state, and marketplace. We conclude our analysis by suggesting how, at each of those levels, women's strategies beyond Cairo will allow us to continue constructing our vision for the future.

Culture and society: challenges ahead

Among the most important achievements of Southern feminists in recent years has been women's impact on changing social norms and practices. Women's organizations have invested a great deal in contesting attitudes about women's and men's confined gender roles and in denouncing the most disturbing manifestations of gender violence – domestic abuse and rape. Transformation of cultural systems that oppress women may be our most challenging task ahead.

Feminist theory and practice in the South must account for the enormous diversity of cultural patterns and gender arrangements throughout the world. Some settings are more favourable to women than others, and most differ significantly from the dominant Western pattern of gender relations. Our challenge, therefore, is to strengthen and support all aspects of cultural transformation and continuity that respect women's integrity without falling into cultural relativism. In all cultures, gender arrangements transform biological differences and sexuality into power relations and human agency. And as Barbieri (1992) observes, 'gender' is a form of social inequality that interacts continuously with class, race and ethnic inequalities in all contexts.

Southern feminists are engaged in three critical areas of research and action to transform gender systems: sexuality, the family and the gender-based boundaries between the private and public spheres. Previously in this volume we noted that sexual representations and practices must be transformed in order effectively to implement the new fertility management policies grounded in rights principles. Although the proposed World Population Plan of Action incorporates a renewed concept of sexuality, the subject is still surrounded by taboos and extreme sensitivities. At the same time, female sexuality has been converted into a battleground where fundamentalist forces are gaining social and political power all over the world. Given this contradictory picture, we must construct a feminist public discourse on women's autonomous sexuality in order to counteract the advances of conservative forces. Similarly, feminist research must go beyond the sexuality–reproductive health and rights nexus in order to examine the threads unifying gender systems, sexuality and the development process.

The same ideology that represses sexuality also 'naturalizes' the family and submits household relationships to a strict model of the Western nuclear family (Jacobson 1992). The Rio Declaration (from the Reproductive Rights and Justice Conference, 1994) proposes a new definition of the family. The Declaration states that there are many forms of family, including families headed by one parent, female or male; extended families; same-sex families and families separated by war and political or economic oppression.

Culturally-defined norms governing sexuality and family structure are linked to the gender categories assigned to the private and public spheres. In most societies, women's activities are confined to the domestic domain, while the public sphere, where the economy, politics and public affairs function, is considered a masculine domain. Since women are actively present in both spheres, feminists have developed a political framework that recognizes the political dimensions of the private sphere (Astelarra 1992). Throughout the South, women are fully integrated in local economies and public community life. They make up the large majority of food producers and are now gradually being incorporated into the 'modern' labour force. Urban and rural women all over the world are engaged in small businesses and trade activities and constitute a large portion of the consumer market. Although Southern women's presence at high levels in politics and public affairs has not improved significantly in the last decade, women's political participation at the community and grassroots levels has expanded enormously (Jain 1994). In most Southern urban settings, for example, women are the primary activists organizing their communities to obtain urban services and food programmes. Feminists must highlight the contributions of grassroots women and inform public opinion of the richness and importance of women's contributions to the construction of civil society in the South.

Beyond Cairo, the international women's movement must sustain and refine its critique of gender arrangements; change public attitudes about female sexuality and the 'ideal' family structure; secure women's rights to social benefits; and advocate the recognition of women's subsistence economic activities and unpaid work in the home. Most important, in their efforts to influence public opinion, women's organizations must consolidate and broaden their participation in public life at local, national and international levels.

State accountability: challenges ahead

The women's movement must now take up the tasks of seeking dialogue with states and organizing to hold national governments accountable for the design and implementation of policies affecting reproductive rights. We must work at two levels – pressing the executive and legislative branches to introduce and ratify policies, and holding the judiciary responsible for upholding national law. Specifically, in addition to providing comprehensive health services (including reproductive health services), governments should be held accountable for taking measures to combat violence against women, female genital mutilation and other practices that are harmful to women.

Policies and programmes should educate and encourage men to take more responsibility for their reproductive behaviour and for transmission of STDs. The policies should comply with international human rights principles, including both first and second generation human rights.

National legal strategies

Building upon the political groundwork of the past two decades, the integration of reproductive rights within the UN Human Rights Charter is now a critical next step in modifying the standard concept of universal human rights.[1] The philosophical and legal bases to support that political struggle are already embedded in the existing

UN instruments. For example, Charlotte Bunch (1993), of the Center for Women's Global Leadership at Rutgers University, maintains that the human rights community must understand fundamentalist attacks on women's integrity not as separate and difficult 'women's issues' but as crucial to the future of human rights. Women's rights should be defended as 'key elements in what human rights will look like in the next century. If the campaign for women's rights as human rights succeeds, women will move to the centre of defining and defending human rights in the next decade.'

International human rights standards may be drawn upon now as a key strategy toward that end, as Florence Butegwa notes:

> The standards set in international treaties and customary law can influence courts at the domestic level. Women's groups are using a country's international obligations as the minimum standard against which national laws should be measured. Gains in this area are slow but significant (Butegwa 1993).

Specific organizing strategies should focus on reproductive rights as intrinsic to the broader Political Rights Covenant's provisions for relations between the state and civil society. The rights to organize politically, to vote and hold public office, and to move freely within national borders must specifically guarantee gender equity. National and international CEDAW agreements also represent indispensable tools for political and legal advancements in reproductive rights. Countries that have ratified CEDAW and/or the International Bill of Rights may be held legally accountable, through international arbitration, for incorporating treaty guarantees into their domestic laws. Local laws and customs that violate the treaties may also be challenged.[2]

Women's reliance upon the recognized human rights framework does not mean it should not be transformed, however, insofar as women's experience of 'rights' suggests a holistic understanding of civil and political rights indivisible from social and economic rights.[3] Transforming the rights discourse and practice will require women's continuous political organizing, including international public solidarity with women who bring cases against their governments.

International legal strategies

Mechanisms for the enforcement of existing human rights and women's rights treaties should be strengthened. The international monitoring committee established by CEDAW is limited in its authority. At present it may only interpret the Convention and receive country reports, but it should also be authorized to investigate complaints and bring actions against governments that condone abuses or do not comply with the Convention.

The UN and other international institutions should be held accountable for monitoring the design and implementation of social and development policies that guarantee women's reproductive rights and health. Mechanisms for regular evaluation should be established and should provide for the participation of women's organizations. In addition, the UN High Commission for Human Rights (established in 1993) should broaden awareness of and compliance with guarantees of women's rights.

Donors and governments should also be held accountable, and their concern for women's health and development should be reflected in their resource allocation and priorities. Donors should revise their funding categories to promote comprehensive women's health programmes rather than narrowly defined family planning programmes. A major requirement is that women-oriented programmes have access to a fair share of the financial resources available.

The marketplace: challenges ahead

Market mechanisms have not proved to be the panacea for social ills that neo-liberal theorists predicted. The devastating worldwide economic crisis has demonstrated that a new balance must be struck between state-managed social and economic development and private initiatives. Women should sound an alarm about reduced state allocations to social sectors and ever-shrinking provision of state services around the world. We must organize against the neo-liberal emphasis on export promotion at the expense of production for local consumption and sustainability. Women should play an active role in identifying alternative development strategies. There is no single blueprint, but any approach must adopt a basic framework of food security, employment and income opportunities and basic services guaranteed through participatory processes.

To understand better the role of market mechanisms in the social sectors of developing economies, we propose that women engage in more research and piloting of public–private partnerships to meet basic needs. Positive experiences should be disseminated across the South, and further comparative South–South research could facilitate mutual communication about the mechanisms that have been effective.

In the area of contraceptive technology, resources should be redirected from provider-controlled and potentially high-risk methods like the vaccine to barrier methods, particularly female-controlled methods that provide both contraception and protection from sexually transmitted diseases, including HIV/AIDS. Women should also monitor the role of multinationals in developing and promoting contraceptives and new reproductive technologies. Medical technology allows women to exercise reproductive decision making, but also submits us to the impersonal and hegemonic forces of medical control. Much of the recent contraceptive and biogenetic research violates the limits of ethical standards, and we must use international scientific ethical principles to monitor such research.[4]

The monitoring process we advocate is a consumer advocacy approach, since women represent the overwhelming majority of consumers of reproductive technologies. At a national level, a minimally democratic context must be in place if a consumer advocacy campaign is to be effective. Consumer advocates organize politically to demand government accountability for assuring that internationally recognized ethical and safety standards are met by companies that test and distribute medical technology.

For example, a new contraceptive method may be tested only among women who fully understand the method's experimental nature, its possible immediate side effects and long-term consequences for their health and fertility.[5] Therefore, governments are responsible for protecting their citizens' safety by regulating both the technology and the system of delivery. In addition to assuming responsibility for ethical testing of new methods, governments are accountable for regulating contraceptive supplies on the market for safety and effectiveness. And finally, private and state services to diagnose women's needs, prescribe and dispense drugs, supplies and procedures (i.e., tubal ligations, assisted fertility, abortions, etc.) are subject to quality and safety standards recognized internationally.

Citizens' groups who feel that state agencies are not complying with official ethical, legal and medical standards to *regulate the quality and safety of reproductive care* may exercise their rights (as provided for in the UN Universal Declaration of Human Rights) to bring legal proceedings against the private manufacturers or government regulatory agencies who do not conform to standards. To increase their influence, women's groups may organize coalitions made up of consumers of medical supplies and services. Since reproductive health affects nearly everyone, broad sectors of civil society – labour unions, teachers' and other professional associations, community-based groups (such as housing advocates, for example), NGOs, churches and other organized groups – may all be convinced to participate in effective coalitions.[6]

When governments or private firms are not responsive to public pressures (due to the failure of democratic processes or a poorly organized civil society), women may appeal to international regulatory standards and legal mechanisms. The World Health Organization, the UN High Commission for Human Rights and the World Court at the Hague, among others, were created to serve as intermediary world bodies that hold states accountable to their citizenry.[7]

Women could use the strategy in cases of particularly egregious offences, such as the marketing of ultrasound technology for sex selection in India. In such cases, members of international feminist and human rights coalitions could organize to pressure their own governments to approve sanctions against offending countries.

DAWN is committed to encouraging women to share their experiences, disseminate information and apply strategies that have worked in very diverse Southern realities. And that has been the purpose of this book, with a focus on how women analyse population dynamics and organize internationally to secure women's reproductive rights and health.

Notes

1. Ramaswamy, cited in Dalcero 1992. Both the Universal Declaration and the Covenants have been faulted for their lack of gender sensitivity, unqualified endorsement of the 'family' as the most important social group, and their failure to articulate women's reproductive rights (See Boland, Rao and Zeidenstein 1994).

2. The broader human rights treaties must be used to challenge laws or seek arbitration, as the international population conference documents do not have such legal binding power.

3. In fact, the original intention of the drafters of the International Covenant on Civil and Political Rights and the International Covenant on Economic, Social and Cultural Rights (both adopted by the UN General Assembly in 1966) was to have a single covenant; they were divided because some of the drafters argued that the two sets of rights would have to be implemented in different ways. Protection of political and civil rights requires only that governments refrain from proscribed action, but realization of economic, social and cultural rights depends on affirmative action and resource commitments by governments. (Together with the 1948 Universal Declaration of Human Rights, the Covenants form the International Bill of Rights.) See Boland, Rao and Zeidenstein 1994.

4. See the Declaration of Ethical Principles, 1994.

5. It is difficult to imagine that poor Southern women (among whom the method is now on trial) can grasp the medical risks involved, since research scientists themselves don't know what the long-term consequences of the vaccine will be. The vaccine is just one example of many medical technologies that are potentially harmful to women. All hormonal methods pose risks to women's health, as do surgical interventions, especially when their irreversibility is poorly understood by consumers.

6. Once a strong coalition of supporters is organized, public interest litigation may be initiated *on behalf of all affected groups, who are represented* by the organized sectors that bring the legal proceedings to court. Such cases, whether against an ineffective government regulatory body or a multinational firm that, for example, markets and distributes hormonal implants irresponsibly, should be surrounded by press and media attention, organized boycotts and public demonstrations. Coalition members should

lobby their elected officials and political candidates to take a public stance on the issue or face a collapse in voter confidence. All of these activities, along with consumers' continued pursuit of legal action, are designed to pressure the private companies or offending government agencies to reform or, if it is necessary to end the abusive practices, to close their doors.

7. The international human rights community provides a recent example of another use of this strategy to apply *external pressures* on governments, in solidarity with internal groups who are protesting abuses. The human rights movement has at least partially succeeded in convincing Northern governments to condition aid allocations or trade agreements to human rights criteria.

Bibliography

Abdullah, H.J. (1992), 'The Relevance of the Concept of Reproductive Rights in the Nigerian Context: some comments' (manuscript).

Abdullah, R. (1993), 'Changing Population Policies and Women's Lives in Malaysia', *Reproductive Health Matters*, No. 1, May.

Adams, A. and Castle, S. (1994), 'Gender Relations and Household Dynamics', in G. Sen, A. Germain and L.C. Chen (eds), *Population Policies Reconsidered: health, empowerment, and rights*, Harvard School of Public Health, Boston.

Akhter, F. (1992), 'The Eugenic and Racist Premise of Reproductive Rights and Population Control', *Issues in Reproductive and Genetic Engineering*, Vol. 5, No. 1, 1–8.

— (1993), 'Report from Population Round Tables', in R.D. Oliveira and T. Corral (eds), *Planeta Fêmea*, Brazilian Women's Coalition, Rio de Janeiro, October.

Alan Guttmacher Institute (1994), 'Aborto Clandestino – Una Realidad Latino Americana', New York.

Aldana, A. (1992), 'Mulher, Sexualidade e Sexo seguro', *Em Tempos de AIDS*, Summus Editorial, São Paulo.

Alencar, J.A. and Andrade, E.C. (1993), 'O Uso de Contraceptivos no Brasil: Uma Análise da Prevalência da Esterilização Feminina', Laboratório Nacional de Computação Científica, No. 4, Rio de Janeiro.

Allen, C. and Bailey, W. (1993), 'A Situational Analysis of Reproductive Health in the Caribbean', Institute of Social and Economic Research, University of the West Indies, draft, Bridgetown, Barbados, October.

Amalric, F. and Banuri, T. (1993), 'Population', draft, June.

Amin, R. Kamal, G.M., Begum, S.F., and Kamal, H. (1989), 'Menstrual Regulation Training and Service Programs in Bangladesh: Results from a National Survey', *Studies in Family Planning*, Vol. 20, No. 2, March, 102–6.

Anand, S. (1994), 'Population, Well-being and Freedom', in G. Sen, A. Germain and L.C. Chen (eds), *Population Policies Reconsidered: health, empowerment, and rights*, Harvard School of Public Health, Boston.

Antrobus, P. (1992), 'Reproductive Right and Health: Reflection on the Road from Rio to Cairo', International Planned Parenthood, Western

Hemisphere Region – Regional Council Meeting, Barbados, August–September (mimeo).

— (1994a), 'DAWN Statement to Plenary', draft prepared at the Third Session Preparatory Committee for ICPD, New York, April.

— (1994b), 'El Ajuste Estructural y la Salud de la Mujer', *Nuestra Voz: población y desarrollo*, Panos Institute, Washington.

Araújo, M.J. (1993), 'Report from Population Round Tables', in R.D. Oliveira and T. Corral (eds), *Planeta Fêmea*, Brazilian Women's Coalition, Rio de Janeiro, October.

Arilha, M. (1993), 'Novas Tecnologias Reprodutivas', *Boletim da Rede Nacional Feminista de Saúde e Direitos Reprodutivos*, Brazil, January.

Ashworth, G. (1993), 'Preparing for the Millennium: Challenge and Change', in J. Kerr (ed.), *Ours by Right: Women's Rights as Human Rights*, Zed Books, London; North-South Institute, Canada.

Asia Indigenous Women's Network (AIWN) and Cordillera Peoples (CPA) (1993), 'II ICPD PREPCOM Statement', presented at the Second Session Preparatory Committee for ICPD, New York, April.

Association of Anti-Prostitution Activity. (1984), 'Anti-prostitution activities in Japan', AAPA, March, (mimeo).

Astelarra, J. (1992), 'Recuperar la Voz: El Silencio de la Cidadania', in R. Rodriguez (ed.), 'Fin de Siglo'; *Genero y Cambio Civilizatorio*. Isis International, Santiago, 47–54.

Ávila, M.B. (1989), 'Direitos Reprodutivos: o Caos e a Ação Governamental', in M.B. Ávila and S. Corrêa (eds), *Os Direitos reprodutivos e a Condição Feminina*, SOS Corpo, Recife.

— (1993), *PAISM: um Programa de Saúde para o Bem Estar de Gênero*. SOS Corpo, Recife, December.

Bakker, M.L. (1991), 'Basic Demographic and Socio-economic Indices of Women in Selected Countries in the South Pacific Region', University of the South Pacific, draft, 27 March.

Bandarage, A. (1994), 'A New and Improved Population Control Policy?', *Political Environments*, No. 1, Committee on Women, Population, and the Environment, spring 1994.

'Bangladesh Country Paper', (1993), presented at the SAARC Ministerial Conference on Women and Family Health, draft, Kathmandu, November.

Barbieri, T. de. (1992), 'Sobre la Categoría de Género: una Introducción Teórico-metodológica', *Revista Interamericana de Sociología*, Vol. VI, No. 2–3, May–December.

— (1993a), 'Breve Resena Acerca de la Política de Población en México', paper presented at the Meeting on Women and Population Policies in

Latin America and the Caribbean, Oaxtepec, Mexico, July.

— (1993b), 'Gender and Population Policies: Some Reflections', *Reproductive Health Matters*, No. 1, May.

Barbosa, R.M. (1992), 'Feminism and AIDS', Seminar on Women and AIDS, Institute of Social Medicine, State University of Rio de Janeiro, June, (mimeo).

Barroso, C. (1991), 'The Impact and Future Directions of Population Program', S/1, March, (mimeo).

— and Corrêa, S. (1990a), 'Os Direitos Reprodutivos na Transição Democrática', prepared for the Symposium of Induced Fertility Change, Bellagio, Italy, February.

— (1990b), 'Public Servants v. Liberal Professionals: The Politics of Contraceptive Research', presented at the Symposium of Induced Fertility Change, Bellagio, Italy, February.

Batliwala, S. (1993), 'Battleground: Women, Population and Reproductive Rights in India', paper prepared for the DAWN Asian Regional Meeting, Singapore, April.

— (1994), 'The Meaning of Women's Empowerment: New Concepts from Action', in G. Sen, A. Germain and L.C. Chen (eds), *Population Policies Reconsidered: health, empowerment, and rights*, Harvard School of Public Health, Boston.

Ben Arrous, M. and Sylva, E. (1991), 'Prostitution: Fillettes de la Rue, Fillettes perdues?', ENDA-INFOP, paper No. 95, 19 March.

Berer, M. (1990a), 'What would a Feminist Population Policy be like?', *Women's Health Journal*, No. 8, April–May–June, 4–7.

— (1990b), 'Reproductive Rights: a Definition and Perspective from the Future', presented at the Plenary 2: Women's Health and Reproductive Rights, 6th International Women and Health Meeting, Quezon City, November, (mimeo).

Berquó, E. (1993a), 'Confrontación Sur-Norte', *Mujeres y Políticas de Población*, Red de Salud de las Mujeres Latinoamericanas y del Caribe/Isis Internacional, Mexico, July.

— (1993b), 'Brasil – Anticoncepção e Partos Cirúrgicos – A espera de uma ação exemplar', *Estudos Feministas*. CIEC/ECO/UFRJ, Vol. 1, No. 2, Rio de Janeiro.

Bhasin, K. and Menon, R. (1988), 'Introduction', *Pressing Against the Boundaries*, draft report of an FAO-FFHC/AD South Asian Workshop on Women and Development, (mimeo).

Bhawan, N. (1993), 'A Population Policy of India', draft, New Delhi, 14 August.

Bianco, M. (1993), 'Políticas de Población: El Caso Argentino', paper presented at the Meeting on Women and Population Policies in Latin America and the Caribbean, Oaxtepec, Mexico, July.

Bledsoe (1987), 'Tinned Milk and Child Fosterage; Side-stepping the Post-partum Sexual Taboo', paper prepared for Rockefeller Conference on the Cultural Roots of African Fertility Regimes, Ife, Nigeria.

Boland, R., Rao, S. and Zeidenstein, G. (1994), 'Honoring Human Rights in Population Policies: from Declaration to Action', in G. Sen, A. Germain and L.C. Chen (eds), *Population Policies Reconsidered: health, empowerment, and rights*, Harvard School of Public Health, Boston.

Bowleg, L. (1992), 'Unjust Punishments: Mandatory HIV Testing of Women Sex Workers and Pregnant Women', Center for Women's Policy Studies, Washington, DC (manuscript).

Brodie, J. (1994), 'Health versus Rights: Comparative Perspectives on Abortion Policy in Canada and the United States', in G. Sen and R. Snow (eds), *Power and Decision: the social control of reproduction*, Harvard University Press, Cambridge, MA .

Brown, B. (1987), 'Facing the "Black Peril": the Politics of the Population Control in South Africa', *Journal of Southern African Studies*, Vol. 13, No. 3, 256–73.

Bruce, J. (1990), 'Fundamental Elements of the Quality of Care: A Simple Framework', in *Studies in Family Planning*, 21 (2): 61–91.

BUKO–Women's Global Network for Reproductive Rights. (1993), 'Call for a halt to research on antifertility "vaccines" (immunological contraceptives)', draft, November.

Bunch, C. (1993), 'Organizing for Women's Human Rights Globally', in J. Kerr (ed.), *Ours by Right: Women's Rights as Human Rights*, Zed Books, London; North-South Institute, Canada.

Butegwa, F. (1992), 'Using the African Charter on Human and People's Rights to Secure Women's access to Land in Africa', paper presented at Consultation on Women's International Human Rights, University of Toronto Faculty of Law.

— (1993), 'The Challenge of Promoting Women's Rights in African Countries', in J. Kerr (ed.), *Ours by Right: Women's Rights as Human Rights*, Zed Books, London; North-South Institute, Canada.

Cabrera, G. (1990), 'Fertility Change in Mexico as Related to Population Policies', paper presented at the Symposium of Induced Fertility Change, Bellagio, Italy, February.

Caldwell, J.C. (1976), 'Towards a Restatement of Demographic Transition Theory', *Population and Development Review*, No. 2.

Canadian International Development Agency (1989), *Population – Research*

Review – Development Special Issue, Canadian International Development Agency, Quebec, February.

Carta de Brasília (1993), Conclusions of the National Meeting on Women and Population: Our Rights for Cairo '94, Brasília, Brazil, September.

Católicas por el Derecho a Decidir (1993), *Estrategias en Salud y Derechos Reproductivos: la Legalización del Aborto en América Latina*, Católicas por el Derecho a Decidir/CDD, Montevideo, Uruguay.

Cho, U. (1993a), 'Global Economy, Industrial Restructuring and Female Labor in Korea: Any Alternative for Development?', paper presented at the DAWN Asian Regional Meeting, Singapore, April.

— (1993b), 'Population and Reproductive Rights in Korea: Issues and Problems Behind Success Story', paper presented at the DAWN Asian Regional Meeting, Singapore, April.

Chung, M. (1991), 'Politics, Tradition and Structural Change: Fijian Fertility in the Twentieth Century', Unpublished Ph.D. thesis, Australian National University.

— (1992), 'Reproductive Rights in the South Pacific', paper presented at the DAWN Regional Pacific Meeting, Suva, Fiji, December.

Coalition Against Trafficking in Women – Asia (1993a), *Women Empowering Women*, Proceedings of the Human Rights Conference on the Trafficking of Asian Women, Coalition Against Trafficking in Women – Asia, Philippines, April.

— (1993b), 'Proposed Convention Against Sexual Exploitation', Coalition Against Trafficking in Women – Asia, draft, Philippines, May.

Committee on Women, Population and the Environment (1993), 'Women, Population and the Environment: Call for a New Approach', Hampshire College, USA (manuscript).

Cook, R. (1992), 'International Protection of Women's Reproductive Rights', *Journal of the International Law and Politics*, Vol. 24, No. 2, Winter.

— (1993), 'The Meaning of Reproductive Rights/Choice/Freedom to Nigerian Women', paper prepared for DAWN African Regional Meeting, Nairobi.

Coomaraswamy, R. (1992), 'To Bellow Like a Cow: Women, Ethnicity and the Discourse of Rights', paper presented at Consultation on Women's International Human Rights, University of Toronto Faculty of Law.

Corrêa, S. (1991), 'Salud de la Mujer: un Panorama Continental', SOS Corpo, Recife, (mimeo).

— (1993), 'Population and Reproductive Rights Component: Platform Document/Preliminary Ideas', Development Alternatives with Women for a New Era – DAWN, Unpublished, February.

— (1994a), 'Esterilización en Brasil: no Exactamente una Opción', *Nuestra Voz: población y desarrollo*, Panos Institute, Washington DC.

— (1994b), 'Relações Desiguais de Gênero e Pobreza', SOS Corpo, Recife, April.

Matamala M., Palomino, N. and Ramos, S. (1994), 'From Paralysis to Fertile Adventures', *DAWN Informs*, No. 1/94, Barbados.

— and Petchesky, R. (1994), 'Reproductive and Sexual Rights: a Feminist Perspective', in G. Sen, A. Germain and L.C. Chen (eds), *Population Policies Reconsidered: health, empowerment, and rights*, Harvard School of Public Health, Boston.

Costa, A.N. (1992), 'O PAISM: Uma Política de Assistência Integral a Saúde da Mulher a ser Resgatada', Comissão de Cidadania e Reprodução, São Paulo.

Cutié Cancino, R. (1993a), 'Reproductive Rights amd Women's Health in Cuba', presented at the DAWN Caribbean Regional Meeting on Reproductive Rights/Population, Barbados, November.

— (1993b), 'El Período Especial de Cuba', in *DAWN Informs*, Bulletin, No. 2/93.

Dacach, S. and Israel, G. (1993), *As Rotas do Norplant: Desvios da Contracepção*, REDEH, Rio de Janeiro.

Dalcero, P. (1992), 'Meio Ambiente e Direitos Humanos numa Sociedade Global', *Proposta*, No. 53, Ano XVI, FASE, Rio de Janeiro, May, 22–7.

DAWN (1993), 'Responses to the Annotated Outline and Recommendations for Improving the Document', drafted at the DAWN Caribbean Meeting on Reproductive Rights and Population, October.

DAWN Panel: 'Women Without Voices' (1994), 'Together Women Speak', Statement produced by DAWN Network at the Third Session Preparatory Committee for ICPD, New York, April, (mimeo).

Davis, A. (1991), 'Outcast Mothers and Surrogates: Racism and Reproductive Politics in the Nineties', in G. Kauffman (ed.), *American Feminist Thought at Century's End: a reader*, Blackwell, Oxford, 1993.

Declaración Andina para una Maternidad sin Riesgos (1993), Conferencia Andina sobre Maternidad sin Riesgos (Bolivia, April), Family Care International, New York.

Declaration of Ethical Principles (1994), Conclusions of the Roundtable on Ethics, Population and Reproductive Health (New York, 8–10 March), Development Law and Policy Program, New York.

Declaration of People's Perspectives on 'Population' (1993), symposium organized by UBINIG and Resistance Network (Bangladesh), Research Foundation for Science and Ecology (India), Third World Network

(Malaysia), and People's Health Network (India), December 12–15, Canilla, Bangladesh.

Degener, T. (1990), 'Female Self-determination between Feminist Claims and 'Voluntary' Eugenics, between "Rights" and Ethics', *Reproductive and Genetic Engineering*, Vol. 3, No. 2, 87–99.

Diagne, S. (1993), 'Defending Women's Rights – Facts and Challenges in Francophone Africa', in J. Kerr (ed.), *Ours by Right: Women's Rights as Human Rights*, Zed Books, London; North-South Institute, Canada.

Diouf, M. and Fatou, S. (no date), 'Etude Prospective: Femmes Sénégalaises à l'Horizon 2015'. République du Sénégal Ministère de la Femme, de L'Enfant et de la Famille, Population Council, draft, Dakar (mimeo).

Dixon-Mueller, R. (1990), 'Abortion Policy and Women's Health in Developing Countries', in *International Journal of Health Services*, Vol. 20, No. 2, 297–314.

— (1993), *Population, Policy and Women's Rights: Transforming Reproductive Choice*, Praeger Publishers, Westport, USA.

Durning, A. (1990), 'Life of the Brink', *Worldwatch*, Vol. 3, No. 2, Washington DC, March-April, 22–30.

Elu, M.C. (1993), 'Abortion yes, Abortion no, in Mexico', *Reproductive Health Matters*, No. 1, May.

Ehrlich, P. and Ehrlich, A. (1990), *The Population Explosion*, Touchstone, New York.

Eshete, A. (1992), 'Population, Women and Development: Gender Issues in the Context of Population and Development', paper prepared for the Conference on Population, Growth and Sustainable Development in Africa: Trends, Issues and Policies, Abidjan, Côte D'Ivoire, September.

Fabros, M.L. (1990), 'The WRRC'S Institutional Framework and Strategies on Reproductive Rights', *Flights 4*, Women's Resource and Research Center, Quezon City, Philippines.

Faria, V. (1989), 'Políticas de Governo e Regulação da Fecundidade', *Ciências Sociais Hoje* – Anuário de antropologia, política e sociologia, Vértice Editora, São Paulo.

Fathalla, M.F. (1994), 'Fertility Control Technology: a Women-Centered Approach to Research', in G. Sen, A. Germain and L.C. Chen (eds), *Population Policies Reconsidered: health, empowerment, and rights*, Harvard School of Public Health, Boston.

Ferringa, B., Iden, S. and Rosenfield, A. (1992), 'Norplant: potential for coercion', in S. Samuels and M. Smith (eds), *Norplant and Poor Women* – Dimensions of New Contraceptives, The Kaiser Forums, sponsored by the Henry J. Kaiser Family Foundation.

Feyisayo, M.A. (1992), 'What Reproductive Rights/Choice/Freedom means to Nigerian Women', paper presented at the EMPARC Forum on Reproductive Rights in the Nigerian Context, University Lagos Guest House, November.

Forte, D.J. (1994), 'Introduction to the DAWN Workshop', paper presented at the DAWN Panel on Sexual and Reproductive Health and Racism, Third Session of the Preparatory Committee for the ICPD, New York, April.

Forum for Women's Health (1993), 'Norplant: Reflections on Some Experiences', Forum for Women's Health, draft, Bombay.

Frasca, T. (1994), 'Sexualidad y Reproducción en el Reino de la Ambiguedad', *Nuestra Voz: población y desarrollo*, Panos Institute, Washington DC.

Freedman, L.P. and Isaacs, S.L. (1993), 'Human Rights and Reproductive Choice', *Studies in Family Planning*, Vol. 24, No. 1, January/February, 18–30.

Fundo das Nações Unidas para a População (1993), *Estado de la Población Mundial*, FUNUAP, New York.

GABRIELA – A National Women's Coalition of Organizations (1993), 'Resolution on Women's Voices 94', Manila, Philippines (manuscript).

García-Moreno, C. and Claro, A. (1994), 'Challenges from the Women's Health Movement: Women's Rights versus Population Control', in G. Sen, A. Germain and L.C. Chen (eds), *Population Policies Reconsidered: health, empowerment, and rights*, Harvard School of Public Health, Boston.

Germain, A. and Ordway, J. (1989), *Population Control and Women's Health: Balancing the Scales*, International Women's Health Coalition, New York.

— and Pitanguy, J. (1993), 'Políticas de Población y Movimiento de Mujeres', *Mujeres y políticas de población*, Red de Salud de las Mujeres Latinoamericanas y del Caribe/Isis Internacional, Mexico, July.

— Nowrojee, S. and Pyne, H.H. (1994), 'Setting a New Agenda: Sexual and Reproductive Health and Rights', in G. Sen, A. Germain and L.C. Chen (eds), *Population Policies Reconsidered: health, empowerment, and rights*, Harvard School of Public Health, Boston.

Gebara, I. (1994), 'Defensa del Aborto en Nombre de la Vida', *Nuestra Voz: población y desarrollo*, Panos Institute, Washington.

Gordon, L. (1976), *Woman's Body, Woman's Right*, Grossman, New York.

Greer, G. (1984), *Sex and Destiny: The Politics of Human Repreduction*, Secker & Warburg, London.

Griffen, V. (1993), 'Women, Population and Development', Notes for the

Pacific Regional Meeting on Population and Development, Port Vila, Vanuatu, September (manuscript).

— (1994), 'Women and Reproductive Rights the Pacific Region', paper prepared for DAWN Inter-regional Meeting on Population and Reproductive Rights, Rio de Janeiro, January.

Guimarães, C.D. (1992), 'Mulheres, Sexualidade e AIDS: A epidemia silenciosa', PRODIR, São Paulo (manuscript).

Gupta, J. (1993), 'People like you never agree to get it: an Indian Family Planning Clinic', in *Reproductive Health Matters*, No. 1, May, 39–43.

Haniff, N.Z. (1992), 'Abortion as a Contraceptive Choice: the Case of Guyana', paper prepared for the Population Council, January.

— (1993), 'The Women's Discourse in Barbados Regarding Reproductive Rights and Population', Report from the DAWN Caribbean Regional Meeting on Reproductive Rights/Population, Barbados, November (mimeo).

Hardon, A. (1993), 'Norplant: Conflicting Views on Safety and Acceptability', in B. Mintzes, A. Hardon and J. Hanhart (eds), *Norplant: Under Her Skin*, Wemos and Women's Health Action Foundation, Amsterdam.

Hartmann, B. (1987), *Reproductive Rights and Wrongs: the global politics of population control and contraceptive choice*, Harper and Row, New York.

— (1993), 'Population Control in the New World Order', in R.D. Oliveira and T. Corral (eds), *Planeta Fêmea*, Brazilian Women's Coalition, Rio de Janeiro.

Hélie-Lucas, M.A. (1993), 'Women Living Under Muslim Laws', in J. Kerr (ed.), *Ours by Right: Women's Rights as Human Rights*, Zed Books, London; North-South Institute, Canada.

Heyzer, N. (1993), 'Market, State and Gender Equity', draft, Kuala Lumpur, Malaysia.

Huq, N. (no date), 'Some Questions on the Norplant Experience in Bangladesh', Naripokkho, draft, Dakar.

Ilumoka, A. (1992), 'African Women's International Economic, Social and Cultural Rights – Toward a Relevant Theory and Practice', paper presented at Consultation on Women's International Human Rights, University of Toronto Faculty of Law.

— (1993), 'The Relevance of Reproductive Rights in the African Context', paper prepared for the Meeting on Reinforcing the Concept of Reproductive Rights, Kovalam, India, May.

Institute of Social Studies Trust (1994), 'Critical Voices for ICPD – Cairo', New Delhi (mimeo).

International Journal of Gynecology and Obstetrics (1989), Supplement 3, 175.

International Women's Health Coalition (1994), *Reproductive Health and Justice, International Women's Health Conference for Cairo '94*, IWHC, New York; Cidadania, Estudos, Pesquisa, Informação, Ação-CEPIA, Rio de Janeiro.

IWRAW (1994), *The Women's Watch*, Vol. 7, No. 3, January.

Jacobson, J. (1992), 'Gender Bias: Roadblock to Sustainable Development', *Worldwatch paper 110*, Worldwatch Institute, Washington DC.

Jain, D. (1994), 'Involuntary Controls – No Place for the 79th Amendment Bill', in *Indian Express*, 2 April, New Delhi (mimeo).

Japan's Network for Women and Health, Cairo '94 (1994), 'Proposal for the Third Preparatory Meeting for the International Conference on Population and Development', Japan's Network for Women and Health, April (manuscript).

Kannabiran, V. (1988), 'Patriarchy', *Pressing Against the Boundaries*, draft report of an FAO–FFHC/AD South Asian Workshop on Women and Development (mimeo).

Keysers, L. and Smyth, I. (1989), 'Family Planning: More than Fertility Control?', Michigan State University.

Kissling, F. (1992), 'Reproductive Rites and Wrongs', *Populi*, No. 15, s/1, July–August.

Klugman, B. (1990), 'The Politics of Contraception in South Africa', *Women's Studies International Forum*, Vol. 13, No. 3, 261–271.

— (1991), 'Population Policy in South Africa: a Critical Perspective', *Development Southern Africa*, Vol. 8, No. 1, February.

Kolder, V.E.B., Gallagher, J. and Parsons, M. (1987), 'Court-ordered Obstetrical Interventions', *New England Journal of Medicine*, No. 316, 1192–96.

Lap-Chew, L. (1994), 'Trafficking in Women: the Experience of the Foundation Against in Women (STV), in the Netherlands', presented at the Reproductive Health and Justice International Women's Health Conference for Cairo '94, Rio de Janeiro, January.

Lateef, S. (1990), 'Women in Development: Solomon Islands', Asian Development Bank, unpublished, November.

— (1991), 'Women in Development: Republic of the Marshall Islands', Asian Development Bank, unpublished, September.

Laureano, S. (1994), 'Sterilization in Puerto Rico: From Massive and Imposed to Wanted and non-Accessible', *Population and Development: We Speak for Ourselves*, Panos Institute, Washington DC.

Lewis, D. and Salo, E. (1993), 'Birth Control, Contraception and Women's Rights in SA', *Agenda*, No. 17.

Lore, C.A. (1993), 'Women and AIDS: Factors that put Women at Risk of

HIV Infection', paper prepared for the African Regional Meeting on Reproductive Rights and Population, Nairobi, Kenya, November.

Louv, R. (no date), 'The Sterilization of American Indian Women', *Esquire*.

McFadden, P. (1992), 'Sex, Sexuality and the Problems of AIDS in Africa', in R. Meena (ed.), *Gender in South Africa: Conceptual and Theorical Issues*, Sapes Books, Harare.

— (1993), Report of the DAWN Regional Meeting held at Nairobi, Kenya, November (manuscript).

McHale, M.C. and Choong, P. (1989), 'A Measure of Humanity', *Futures*, February.

MacKinnon, C.A. (1992), 'Reflections on Sex Equality under Law', in L.S. Kauffman (ed.), *American Feminist Thought at Century's End: A reader*, Blackwell, Oxford, 1993.

Madunagu, B. (1993), in 'Report from Population Round Tables', *Planeta Fêmea*, Brazilian Women's Coalition, Brazil, October.

— (1994), 'The Minority Question: the Nigerian Experience', paper presented at the DAWN Panel on Sexual and Reproductive Health and Racism, Third Session of the Preparatory Committee for the ICPD, New York, April.

Mahmud, S. and Johnston, A.M. (1994), 'Women's Status, Empowerment, and Reproductive Outcomes', in G. Sen, A. Germain and L.C. Chen (eds), *Population Policies Reconsidered: health, empowerment, and rights*, Harvard School of Public Health, Boston.

Makatini, L. (1993), 'Abortion as a Human Rights Issue', *Agenda*, No. 17.

Manana, T. (1992), 'Conventional Economic Theories and Gender Analysis', in R. Meena (ed.), *Gender in South Africa: Conceptual and Theoretical Issues*, SAPES Books, Harare.

Manguyu, F.W. (1994), 'Key Issues for Women Organizing for Reproductive Health and Justice', issues raised at the First Regional Congress of the Near East and Africa Region of the Medical Women's International Association (MWIA), on the Health of Women and Safe Motherhood, Nairobi, Kenya, November–December (manuscript).

Mann, J., Piot, P. and Quinn, T. (1988), 'The International Epidemiology of AIDS', *Scientific American*, Vol. 259, No. 4, October, 82–89.

Marcelo, A.B. (1993), 'Population Policy and Program Development in the Philippines: Actors, Issues, and Gaps', paper presented at DAWN Asian Regional Meeting, Singapore, April.

Matamala, M. (1993), 'Foro Abierto de Salud y Derechos Reproductivos en Chile: una Estrategia', paper prepared for the Meeting on Women and Population Policies in Latin America and the Caribbean, Oaxtepec, Mexico, July.

Mazrui, A.A. (1990), 'Islamic Doctrine and the Politics of Induced Fertility Change: an Africa Perspective', paper presented at The Politics of Induced Fertility Change, sponsored by the University of Michigan, Rockefeller Center, Bellagio, Italy, February.

Merrick, T.W. (1990), 'The World Bank and Population: Case Studies of Fertility Decline in Brazil, Colombia and Mexico', The Population Reference Bureau, draft, Washington, DC, October.

Mertens, W. (1993), 'Population Growth and Economic Development', (manuscript).

Mintzes, B., Hardon, A. and Hanhart, J. (eds) (1993), *Norplant: Under Her Skin*, Women and Pharmaceuticals Project, Women's Health Action Foundation and WEMOS. Eburon, Delft, The Netherlands.

Mukherjee, V.N. (1993), *Shaping a Better Future: Women's Perspectives on Alternative Economic Framework and Population and Reproductive Rights*, Report of The DAWN/APCD Asian Regional Meeting on Population, Gender and Sustainable Development (Singapore, 12–14 April), Asian and Pacific Development Centre-APDC, Kuala Lumpur, Malaysia.

Nagaoki, S. (1993), 'What Can be Seen from a Country Experiencing Population Decrease', Report for International Symposium People's Perspective on Population, Japan (mimeo).

Nair, S. (1993), 'Reproductive Rights – A Slogan Appropriate for Indian Women?', paper presented at International Conference on Reinforcing Reproductive Rights, Women's Global Network for Reproductive Rights, Madras, India, May.

Nanne, K. and Bergamo, M. (1993), 'Aborto não é Pecado', interview with Ivone Gebara, *Veja*, 6 October, 7–9.

NGO Treaty on Population and Environment (1993), In R.D. Oliveira and T. Corral (eds), *Planeta Fêmea*, Brazilian Women's Coalition, Rio de Janeiro, October.

Obermeyer, C.M. (1994), 'Reproductive Choice in Islam: Family, State, and Women's Options', in G. Sen and R. Snow (eds), *Power and Decision: the social control of reproduction*, Harvard University Press, Cambridge, MA.

O'Leary, S. and Cheney, B. (1993), *Tripla Ameaça: AIDS e Mulheres – Dossiê Panos* (translation: Ana Dourado) Panos Institute, London; ABIA, Rio de Janeiro; SOS Corpo, Recife.

Omigbodun, A.O. (1993), 'The Burden of Reproductive Tract Infections on Nigerian Women', paper presented at the workshop on Reproductive Tract Infections in Nigerian Women, University of Ibadan, Ibadan, May.

Organization of Africa Unity (1993), 'Report of the Secretary General on the Six Action Point Agenda of the Declaration of AIDS Epidemic in

Africa: progress report and guidelines for action', Council of Ministers Fifty-eight Ordinary Session, CM/1780(LVIII), Cairo, Egypt, 21–26 June.

Orubuloye, I.O. , Caldwell, P. and Caldwell, J.C. (1993), 'The Role of High-risk Occupations in the Spread of AIDS: truck drivers and itinerant market women in Nigeria', *International Family Planning Perspectives*, Vol. 19, No. 2, June, 43–48.

Pacific Island States. (1993), 'Port Vila Declaration on Population and Sustainable Development', Pacific Island States, Port Vila, Vanuatu, September (mimeo).

Palomino, N. (1993), 'Puntos de Encuentro con Mujeres Urbano-populares en Salud, Sexualidad y Derechos Reproductivos', paper presented at the Meeting on Women and Population Policies in Latin America and the Caribbean, Oaxtepec, Mexico, July.

Patel, R. (1993), 'Challenges Facing Women in Pakistan', in J. Kerr (ed.), *Ours by Right: Women's Rights as Human Rights*, Zed Books, London; North-South Institute, Canada.

Perera, M. (1993), 'Alternative Economic Framework' – Sri Lanka Country paper (manuscript), paper prepared for the DAWN Asian Regional Meeting on Population, Reproductive Rights and an Alternative Development Framework, Singapore, April.

Petchesky, R.P. (1990), *Abortion and Women's Choice: the State, Sexuality and Reproductive Freedom*. Northeastern University Press, Boston, MA.

— and Weiner, J. (1990), 'Global Feminist Perspective on Reproductive Rights and Reproductive Health', Report on the Special Session Held at the Fourth International Interdisciplinary Congress on Women, Hunter College, New York, June (mimeo).

Pettiti, D. (1992), 'Issues in Evaluating Norplant', in S. Samuels and M. Smith (eds), *Norplant and Poor Women*, The Kaiser Forums, sponsored by the Henry J. Kaiser Family Foundation.

Pizarro, A.M. (1993), 'Actuales Políticas de Población Mundial: Actuales Políticas de Población en Nicaragua', presented in the Encuentro Nacional de Mujeres sobre Políticas de Población y Desarrollo, Ministerio de Acción Social, Managua, Nicaragua, December (mimeo).

Phizacklea, A. (1994), 'Women and International Migration: Health-related Issues', paper prepared at the Reproductive Health and Justice International Women's Health Conference for Cairo' 94, Rio de Janeiro, January.

Potter, J.E., Mojaro, O. and Nunez, L. (1987), 'The Influence of Health Care on Contraceptive Acceptance in Rural Mexico', *Studies in Family Planning*, Vol. 18, No. 3, May–June.

Priso Jeanne, D. (1994a), 'Contribution au Débat sur les Politiques de Population', paper prepared for DAWN Inter-regional Meeting Population and Reproductive Rights, Rio de Janeiro, January.

— (1994b), 'Sur Population de L'Afrique: Mythes et Réalités', paper presented at the DAWN Panel on Sexual and Reproductive Health and Racism, Third Session of the Preparatory Committee for the ICPD, New York, April.

Pyne, H.H. (1994), 'Reproductive Experiences of Needs of Thai Women: Where has Development Taken Us?', in G. Sen and R. Snow (eds), *Power and Decision: the social control of reproduction*, Harvard University Press, Cambridge, MA.

Raharjo, Y. (1993), 'Population Policies, Reproductive Health and Reproductive Rights: Indonesian Case', paper presented at the DAWN Regional Meeting, Singapore, April.

Ramos, S. and Viladrich, A. (1993), *Abortos Hospitalizados: Entrada y Salida de Emergencia*, Documentos CEDES/88, serie Salud y Sociedad, Centro de Estudios de Estado y Sociedad-CEDES, Buenos Aires.

Ravindran, T.K.S. (1993), 'The Politics of Women, Population and Development in India', *Reproductive Health Matters*, No. 1, May.

Ribeiro, L.C. (no date), 'A Experiência do Aborto entre Mulheres Católicas', ISER, Rio de Janeiro (manuscript).

Roland, E. (1994), 'Reproductive Rights and Racism in Brazil: the Dilemma of the Tostines Crackers', paper presented at the DAWN Panel on Sexual and Reproductive Health and Racism, Third Session of the Preparatory Committee for the ICPD, New York, April.

Ross, A.J., Mauldin, W.P. and Miller, V.C. (1993), *Family Planning and Population: a Compendium of International Statistics*, Population Council, New York.

Ross, L.J. (1993a), 'Reproductive Rights and African American Women', draft, Georgia, May.

— (1993b), Center for Democratic Renewal, Washington DC (unpublished manuscript).

Rousselle, A. (1980), *PORNÉIA*, Editora Graal, Rio de Janeiro.

Saman, S. (no date), 'Is There a Need for a Population Program for South Africa? Political Implications of a Population Development Program', paper presented at the Pan Africanist Congress of Azania.

Scott, J. (1992a), 'Norplant and Women of Color', in S. Samuels and M. Smith (eds), *Norplant and Poor Women*, The Kaiser Forums, sponsored by the Henry J. Kaiser Family Foundation.

— (1992b), Written Testimony on the Use of Depo Provera in the United

States as a Contraceptive Before the Food and Drug Administration Fertility and Maternal Health Drugs Advisory Committee, 19 June.

Sen, A. (1990), 'More than 100 Million Women are Missing', *New York Review of Books*, 20 December.

Sen, G. (1993a), 'Alternative Economic Framework', in V.N. Mukherjee *Shaping a Better Future*, Asian and Pacific Development Centre – APDC, Kuala Lumpur, Malaysia.

— (1993b), 'Women's Empowerment and Human Rights: the Challenge to Policy', paper presented at the Population Summit of the World's Scientific Academies, New Delhi, October.

— (1994), 'Development, Population, and the Environment: a Search for Balance', in G. Sen, A. Germain and L.C. Chen (eds), *Population Policies Reconsidered: health, empowerment, and rights*, Harvard School of Public Health, Boston.

— and Grown, C. (1987), *Development, Crisis and Alternative Visions – Third World Women's Perspectives*, Monthly Review Press, New York.

Shane, N. (1993), 'AIDS Alive!', *The Weekender*, 20 August, 6–7.

Shanter, A.F. (1992), 'Contraceptive Vaccines: Promises and Problems', in H.B. Holmes (ed.), *Issues in Reproductive Technology I: an anthology*, Garland, New York.

Shiva, V. (1993), 'The Strong, the Weak, the Wounded: an unacceptable triangle', in R.D. Oliveira and T. Corral (eds), *Planeta Fêmea*, Brazilian Women's Coalition, Rio de Janiero.

Siddiqi, N. (1993), 'Population, Reproduction, and Development: a Different Perspective', paper presented at the DAWN Asian Regional Meeting, Singapore, April.

Simmons, R., Koenig, M.A. and Zahidul Huque, A.A. (1990), 'Maternal-child Health and Family Planning: User Perspectives and Service Constrains in Rural Bangladesh', *Studies in Family Planning*, Vol. 21, No. 4, July–August.

Smyth, I. (1991), 'The Indonesian Family Planning Program: a Success Story for Women?', *Alternatives*, Vol. 16, 781–805.

Southern NGO Caucus (1993), 'Areas of Concerns: Southern NGO Statement to all Participants in the ICPD Process', Second Preparatory Committee for the ICPD, New York, April.

Sundstrom, K. (1993), 'Unplanned Pregnancies and Abortion', World Bank, draft, Washington DC.

Thomas, D.Q. (1993), 'Holding Governments Accountable by Public Pressure', in J. Kerr (ed.), *Ours by Right: Women's Rights as Human Rights*, Zed Books, London; North-South Institute, Canada.

UBINIG (no date), 'The Price of Norplant is tk 2, 000. You cannot remove it. The clients are refused removal in Norplant Trial in Bangladesh', Boston Women's Health Book Collective Center (mimeo).

United Nations (1992a), Economic and Social Council, attachment 3– recommendations, part of E/Conf. 84/PC/7, 3 November. (United Nations Expert Group Meeting on Family Well-being, Bangalore, 26– 30 October).

— (1992b), 'Draft Recommendations. United Nations Experts Groups Meeting on Population and Women', Gaborone, June.

— (1993a), 'Proyecto de Marco Conceptual para la Formulación de las Recomendaciones de la Conferencia', E/CONF. 84/PC/L. 9. Apresentado por el Presidente del Comité Preparatorio sobre las bases de consultas oficiosas, Second Preparatory Session for ICPD, 20 May.

— (1993b), 'Chairman Summary of the Conceptual Framework' – Second Session of the Preparatory Committee – May, New York.

— (1993c), General Assembly, A/48/150, 'Annotated outline of the final document of the Conference', note by the Secretary-General, 21 September.

— (1994a), 'Draft Final Document of the Conference', A/CONF. 171/ PC/5, Programme of Action of the Conference, note by the Secretary-General, 4 January.

— (1994b), 'Draft Final Document of the Conference', 13 May, disseminated by the electronic Conference ICPD, General/NGONET.

United Nations Fund for Population Activities (1991), 'Statement on Population and Environment', issued by participants of UNFPA'S Expert Meeting on Population and Environment UN Headquarters, New York, 4–5 March.

— (1993a), Estado de la Población Mundial, UN, New York.

— (1993b), The Fourth Pacific Islands Conference of Leaders, Tahiti, French Polynesia, 24–25 June.

U.S. Women of Color Coalition for Reproductive Health and Rights (1994), U.S. Women of Color Delegation to the ICPD (manuscript).

Van Anh, T.T. (1993), 'Population Policies and the Process of Economic Renovation in Vietnam', paper prepared for the DAWN Asian Regional Meeting, Singapore, April.

Wajcman, J. (1994), 'Delivered Into Men's Hands? The Gender Relations of Reproductive Technology', in G. Sen and R. Snow (eds), Power and Decision: the social control of reproduction, Harvard University Press, Cambridge, MA.

Ward, S., Sigit Sidi I., Simmons, R. and Simmons G. (1990), 'Service Delivery Systems and Quality of Care in Implantation of Norplant', report prepared for the Population Council.

Warwick, D. (1988), 'Culture and the Management of Family Planning Programs', *Studies in Family Planning*, Vol. 19, No. 1, 1–18.

Wiltshire, R. (1992), *Environment and Development: Grass Roots Women's Perspective*, DAWN, Barbados.

Women's Declaration on Population Policies (1993), in Preparation for the 1994 International Conference on Population and Development (1993), DAWN (Barbados), Reproductive Health Matters (London), Latin American and Caribbean Women's Health Network (Santiago), National Feminist Health and Reproductive Rights Network (Recife), IWHC (New York), OXFAM Health Unit Coordinator (Oxford), Women Living Under Muslim Laws International Solidarity Network (Grabels), Gender and Development Programme Asian and Pacific Development Centre (Kuala Lumpur), Bangladesh Women's Health Coalition (Dhaka), Safe Motherhood Office – World Bank (Kampala), WGNRR (Amsterdam), Catholics for Free Choice (Washington), WIN (Calabar), Medical Women's International (Nairobi), Institute for Social Studies & Action and Women Health Philippines (Quezon City), Uganda National Council of Women and Organizing Committee for 7th International Women's Health Meeting (Kampala), Kenya Medical Women's Association (Nairobi), IRRRAG (New York), CEPIA (Rio de Janeiro), Rural Women's Social Education Centre (Tamil Nadu), National Black Women's Health Project (Washington, DC), and Association of Women for Action and Research (Singapore), March.

Women's Global Network for Reproductive Rights (1993a), 'International Conference Reinforcing Reproductive Rights', discussion paper, WGNRR, Madras, India, May (mimeo).

— (1993b), 'Population and Development Policies', WGNRR Newsletter 43, April–June.

— (1993c), 'Report of the International Conference "Reinforcing Reproductive Rights", (Madras, India, 5–8 May 1993)', WGNRR, India, May.

World Bank (1988), 'Indonesia: Family Planning Perspectives in the 1990's', World Bank Country Study, Washington, DC.

— (1993), *World Development Report 1993*, World Bank, Washington, DC, July.

World Health Organization/Special Programme of Research, Development and Research Training in Human Reproduction (UNDP, UNFPA, WHO, World Bank) (1992a), 'An extract from: Reproductive health: a key to a brighter future', Biennial Report 1990–1991. Special 20th anniversary issue, World Health Organization, Geneva.

— (1992b), *Orientame: Embarazo Indeseado y Aborto*, WHO, Bogotá.

Wright, R. (1994), 'Um Explosivo Exército de Esquecidos', *Jornal do Brasil*, 20 March, 15.

Zeitlin, J. , Govindaraj, R. and Chen. L.C. (1994), 'Financing Reproductive and Sexual Health Services', in G. Sen, A. Germain and L.C. Chen (eds), *Population Policies Reconsidered: health, empowerment, and rights*, Harvard School of Public Health, Boston.

Index

aboriginal women, in Australia, 44
abortion, 3, 10, 17, 27, 39, 42, 56, 60,
  65, 68–73, 74, 78, 82, 110; after
  Russian Revolution, 11; as
  epidemiological problem, 69; as
  resistance to slavery, 68;
  clandestine, 40; illegal, 29, 40, 70,
  85; in Cuba, 11; in US, 72; legal,
  11, 58, 65, 69, 72; legal status of,
  70; legalization of, 45, 71;
  opposition to, 73; post-
  amniocentesis, 79; promotion of, 70;
  rates in Chile, 41; rights, 67;
  techniques, 91; treatment for, 87;
  unsafe, 7
adultery, killing of women for, 56
advocacy groups, 4
Afghanistan, 32
African-American activism, 44
AIDS, 68, 87; and sex industry, 74; as
  rights issue, 73–6; diagnosis of, 65;
  protection from, 109; vaccine
  tested, 89; women and, 44
Algeria, 32, 56, 79
amniocentesis, and gender choice, 79,
  89–90, 91
apartheid, 25, 42
Argentina, 25, 41
Arilha, Margareth, 91
armed conflict, effects on women, 9
Australia, 59

baby boom, 10
Bangladesh, 16, 21, 24, 25, 26, 28, 32,
  33, 78, 79, 85, 90
basic needs approach, 25, 45, 46, 98
Bill of Rights, International, 107
biogenetic research, and violation of
  ethics, 109
body, integrity of, 77
Bolivia, 16, 21

Botswana, 34
Brazil, 17, 18, 21, 24, 37–40, 56, 85,
  87, 89, 90, 91, 92; abortion rates in,
  40; caesarean sections in, 39, 90
breastfeeding facilities, 87
Bretton Woods institutions, 48
bride price, 83
Bruce, Judith, 86
Bunch, Charlotte, 107
Butegwa, Florence, 107

caesarean sections, 89; in Brazil, 39, 90
Cambodia, 16, 41
Cameroon, 43
cancer: prevention of, 7, 58, 91;
  screening for, 86
care, quality of, 86, 110
Catholic Church, 3, 11, 17, 38, 70, 73
Central African Republic, 34
Chad, 34
child care, 7, 59; centres, 87; men and,
  42; sharing of, 81
child marriage, 82, 83
childbearing, incapacity of, 82
children: fostering of, 34; number and
  spacing of, 3, 36, 67
Chile, 15, 25, 41; abortion rate in, 41
China, 12, 14, 16, 24, 25, 26, 70, 78, 79
Christianity *see* fundamentalism
coalitions, building of, 63, 110
Colombia, 21, 22, 24, 37–40
colonialism, 6, 13
combined policies of population
  management, 37–40
communications systems, effect on
  cultural norms, 37
community-based distribution (CBD)
  of contraception, 17–18
condoms, men's attitude to, 27, 39, 75
contraception, 1, 16, 25, 37, 62, 79;
  choice of methods, 86; development